The History Of Horsley

Ready. handwritten: Rd, Feb. 3. '95

Now Ready, Crown 8vo. 74 pp., Price 2/- nett.

Illustrated by Three Heliotype Prints and Eight Chalk

Drawings.

THE

HISTORY OF HORSLEY.

BY THE

REV. MESSING RUDKIN.

VICAR;

DEDICATED BY PERMISSION TO

COLONEL KINGSCOTE, C.B., M.P.,

IN GRATEFUL REMEMBRANCE OF MANY KIND DEEDS

DONE BY HIM;

AND WITHOUT PERMISSION TO

THE

HISTORY OF HORSLEY,

BY THE

REV. MESSING RUDKIN,

VICAR;

ᴅᴇᴅɪᴄᴀᴛᴇᴅ ʙʏ ᴘᴇʀᴍɪꜱꜱɪᴏɴ ᴛᴏ

COLONEL KINGSCOTE, C.B., M.P.,

IN GRATEFUL REMEMBRANCE OF MANY KIND DEEDS
DONE BY HIM;

AND WITHOUT ᴘᴇʀᴍɪꜱꜱɪᴏɴ ᴛᴏ

THE PEOPLE OF HORSLEY.

Illustrated by Sundry Views.

PRICE 2/-

DURSLEY:
WHITMORE AND SON, LETTERPRESS AND LITHOGRAPHIC PRINTERS.

1884.

DURSLEY:

WHITMORE AND SON, STEAM PRINTERS, LONG STREET.

PREFACE.

———o———

The following pages contain the substance of a lecture given at the Nailsworth Institute in the month of January, 1883, with subsequent corrections and additions.

The information here presented has been gathered from very many sources too numerous to mention, and care has been taken to make it as accurate as possible.

Other sources of information remain unexplored. A search at the British Museum for old deeds belonging to the Abbey of Bruton and the Priory of Horsley might not be unsuccessful. And the Diocesan Registry of Worcester, and also that of Gloucester, and the Public Record Office, would, if searched, undoubtedly yield valuable sources of information. Then again, an examination of the deeds belonging to the Lord of the Manor would throw much light on the later history of the parish. And there are sermons in stones yet to be read—the stones being yet buried—for in several places there are apparently signs of primitive remains which have not yet been examined.

Perhaps some other worker at a future day may give a more complete history of the parish. Meanwhile the present writer commits these pages to the press, hoping that to the people of Horsley they may prove interesting.

At the same time he takes the opportunity of thanking the many friends who have kindly helped in giving him information, and his thanks are especially due to Miss Mason, of Shortwood, for the execution of the Sketches which illustrate this book.

Horsley Vicarage,
   November 30th, 1884.

List of Illustrations.

PAGE

HORSLEY.

HORSLEY is a large parish extending from six to seven miles in length and from three to four in breadth. It is bounded on the North and East by the parish of Avening; on the South-East and South by Tetbury, Beverston, and Bagpath; on the South-West by Kingscote; on the West by Nympsfield; and on the North-West it is just touched by Woodchester. Its boundaries do not follow any natural lines of division, but evidently coincide with the limits of the Ancient Manor, the Ancient Manor being the extent of a private property.

The name Horsley was written in early times Horkesleigh or Hurstleigh. *Hurst* is the Anglo-Saxon name for a wood, and the termination *leigh* or *ley* may be derived from a British word *lle*, signifying a place, or from the Anglo-Saxon *leug* or *leigh* a field or pasture. This latter word is apparently sometimes used for a wood. I notice the application of the name to the woods opposite Clifton and known as the Leigh Woods. Horsley therefore may mean the wooded place, or field, or be simply a duplicate name, both parts of which mean a wood. In either case the name reveals to us the nature of the parish in those ancient times, and even in the present day it is not inappropriate. Rudder, who wrote a History of Gloucestershire a little over 100 years ago, says of Horsley: "There are in this parish, more especially where some of the houses are built, several dingles and narrow bottoms with hanging woods and verdant steeps, which give it a romantic appearance not easy to be described." In this record we have a picture of what Horsley is also to-day. Some of the woods have indeed been

B

cut down in recent years, but still the parish has a wooded aspect [1]
and romantic appearance, which give it a charm quite irresistible,
and provocative of the admiration of all strangers. We go to
Westmoreland or Wales in search of fine scenery and we find it
on a larger scale, but I venture to think we get nothing more
picturesque that what we have at our own doors.

Seeing what Horsley is to-day we may very easily picture what it
was like in primitive times. I imagine our hill-sides were clothed
everywhere with woods of beech, interspersed with Scotch fir, and
oak and hazel nut. The narrow bottoms were swamps covered by
dense thickets of alders and willows giving shelter to numerous
red-deer and beavers, whose remains have been dug up in neighbouring bottoms in recent times, and even to-day adorn the
Museum of this Nailsworth Institute. On the hill tops there were
some open spaces partaking of the nature of moor or common,
particularly on the high ground reaching from Barton End to
Cranmore.

<h3 style="text-align:center">ANCIENT WAYS.</h3>

There were ancient ways or tracks crossing this wild forest
country, yet not in the direction of the highways which are so
prominent to-day. The Bath and Bristol roads did not exist
in those early days. The traffic did not then flow from North to
South as now, but from West to East. The great thoroughfares
did not cross the Parish as now, but followed its length. The chief
highway now known as the Bristol Road was only begun to be made
by being cut in many places through the solid rock, in the year
1800. An entry in one of our parish registers, by the hand of the
Rev. Dudley Fosbrook is sufficient proof of this. The Bath Road
was made about the same date or later. Obliterate these two
great thoroughfares from the mental view and what a different place
Horsley becomes. I am told that an ancient writing belonging
to a property situated at Horsley Street, and which formerly
belonged to Mr. Thomas Bird, but is now part of our school
property, described the property as situated—not as we might
suppose on the highway leading to Bristol—but on the road leading
from Nympsfield to Tiltups End and Tetbury. And on examining
the map it will be seen that in early times this was probably one of
the most important thoroughfares in this part of the country. It
was the nearest route from South Wales. Leaving Newnham

[1] Since this was written, the Beech Wood, known as the Park Wood has been cut down.

Passage it passed by Fretherne, Frampton, Alkerton, and Frocester, over Frocester hill, not by the line of the present road, but by the old way still to be seen going up in zigzag fashion through the wood and coming out not far from the present entrance to Woodchester Park. Then the road passes through the village of Nympsfield by Field Farm until it approaches the village of Horsley by the place now known as the "Ragged." Perhaps in earlier times, when this road was used more than it is now, an Inn bearing this name was found there. The road would next pass through Nup End and Horsley proper, and down the hill to Hartley Bridge and up the steep ascent of Hay Lane and on to Chavenage and Tetbury and the regions beyond. I shall have occasion to refer to this ancient way again, when we reach the times of Cromwell.

Another ancient way I conceive to be that which branches out of the former at the village of Horsley, and then descends with great steepness to the Washpool and continues under the name of Barton End Lane, until it crosses the Bath Road just by the back of the residence of the late Mrs. Wood, and continues over the ridge by Hazlewood to Avening and in the direction of Cirencester.

There was another ancient way which may still be traced coming up from Gloucester through the parish of Woodchester by the hill side to Forest Green, where it dipped across the valley at Nailsworth and went up by what is still called Tetbury Lane to the back of Barton End, where it crosses the way last spoken of leading from Horsley to Avening, and then goes on by Ledgemore bottom to Chavenage and Tetbury.

Another way there must have been, if not in the very primitive times, yet in later years, going up from Nailsworth, at what point I cannot exactly say, and after following the summit of the ridge we call Rockness, either dipped down as now under the "Grove" in which the Vicarage is built, or as I strongly suspect passed as a mere track above the Vicarage by what is still called "The Ridings" into Downend and then up the hill by Horsley Court till it met the two ways leading respectively to Avening and to Tetbury.

When one reflects that the present highway or highways leading out of Nailsworth to Horsley were not in existence until the beginning of this century, for it seems that until then neither the upper nor the lower road was made, we can see what a rough and steep and perilous route it must have been for the traveller, and not lightly to be followed. But in those days there was little vehicular traffic, and so the roughness of the road did not so much matter. Still a tradition seems to linger in Horsley that in early times the traveller wishing to pass the village from Nailsworth preferred to go by way of Tetbury Lane to the back of Barton End and then by the Barton End Lane to the Washpool.[1] Travellers say many of the roads in Norway follow the beds of the water courses, and such is the case at Horsley. The road which leads from Downend to the Washpool still follows the watercourse. The cart road is the bed of the stream. And the road leading from the Washpool to Barton End was evidently in ancient times nothing better than the bed of a watercourse. At the present day the water has been diverted by artificial channels across the fields above for the purposes of irrigation, whence it falls about half way up the lane in a pretty cascade, emulating in the rainy weather even the waterfalls of Wales. At such seasons also in defiance of highway surveyor and waywardens it will assert its ancient rights, and rushes down the lane with such force as to tear up the causeway and quite stop the foot traffic. The great depth of the lane below the level of the adjacent lands bears witness to the work done by it in the ages past.

A BATTLE FIELD.

This lane as previously mentioned is one of the ancient ways leading from the Severn into the heart of England. In primitive times its steep slopes on both sides were doubtless clothed with wood of beech, down to the very roadway. Even now the beech wood for some part of the way comes very near to it. I will describe what I imagine to have happened in that lane at a remote period. Up the ancient track and under cover of the woods an invading foe advances. They ascend the track and

---

1 In a book entitled "A Tour to Cheltenham Spa, or Gloucestershire Displayed," published 1803—The Itinerary from Bath to Cheltenham gives the various stages as follows :—

		Miles.		Furlongs.	
Lasborough ...	...	4	...	0	(from Dunkirk.)
Kingscote Inn	...	1	...	0	
Tipput's Inn	...	1	...	0	
Horsley	...	1	...	0	
Nailsworth ...	...	1	...	0	
Inchborough...	...	1	...	3	
Rodborough ...	...	2	...	0	
Stroud	...	...	0	...	6

It seems from the above, that the route was not the same as now, and evidently at that date the Bath Road was not made. The road probably was from Kingscote, by Hazlecote, to Tipputs Inn, and then by Hay Lane to Horsley. The stage from Nailsworth was to Inchborough, or Inchbrook—one mile and three furlongs. Tipputs Inn may have been the origin of the present name Tiltups End.

have well nigh reached the open country above when their progress is opposed. Another band of warriors occupy the heights just above Barton End House. But nothing daunted, the invading force continues its way and climbs those heights, and there follows a great battle. Tokens of the bloody fight are found even in the present day. A human skull and a jawbone, fractured as by club and spear, have been dug out quite recently in the garden of "The Retreat." And at various times in recent years other human remains have been disinterred. And old people speak of human remains and weapons having been dug up frequently in the fields adjoining and even right away as far as Hazlewood. Probably a great battle was fought there. But when was it fought? And who where the Combatants? It might have been an invading force of Britons coming up from the fastnesses of Wales and seeking to recover lost territory from the encroaching power of Rome. Or it might have been a fight between Saxon and Saxon. Or a band of Danes coming up from the banks of the Severn to make a raid against the Saxons. But at some period previous to the Norman Invasion must this battle be ascribed. I am inclined to fix its date in very early times, because of the many primitive remains which are still found on the level country beyond, and which it may be are memorials of the event.

The ridge above Barton End is the second that would be encountered by any invading force coming up from the Severn by the route before described. And while the ridge, of which Frocester Hill forms part, is covered with primitive remains, so is this second ridge. Ascending the lane beyond "The Retreat" we reach the open country. On the left we pass the ancient way coming up from Nailsworth. A little further we come to the cross roads, the left hand going to Avening, through Hazlewood, in which have been found ancient British Barrows, and the right hand will take us to Chavenage. As the road turns towards Chavenage, by the road side on the right we pass Shipton's grave : he was a suicide buried here in unhallowed ground, in accordance with the bygone custom. The road now enters a large field in which as the ordnance map shows there stood very lately an ancient monument called the Picked Stone.

THE PICKED STONE.

The stone occupied the highest spot on the hill, and in the days before the country was enclosed must have been a notable landmark. It stood about four feet from the ground, and seems to have been

in character not unlike the Long Stone at Minchinhampton. Was
it a mere landmark? or did it denote the site of an ancient battle
field, for a battle field there was certainly not far away? or was it set
up over the grave of some eminent chieftain? or was it connected
with the worship of the Druids? This stone seems to have received a
certain superstitious regard from the old inhabitants of Horsley.
There are persons still living who have told me that in the days of
their childhood they frequently visited it, to wait for the marvellous
phenomenon, which tradition said, might be observed of the stone
walking round the field when the clock struck twelve. But men of
this utilitarian age, begrudged the bit of ground on which this
stone stood, and some forty years ago it was by sacrilegious hands
removed and broken up, and built into some granary steps in a
farmyard not far away.

BRITISH BARROWS.

Mourning over this act of vandalism we follow our road. The
ordnance map again shows that across a field to the left are the
remains of ancient tumuli, and these grave mounds are still plainly
seen—but they have been opened. A good account of them is
found in a paper written by the late Mr. G. F. Playne for the
Cotswold Naturalists' Field Club, from which I now quote: "The
Lechmore Tumulus contained so recently as 1812 one chamber, but
the stones of which it was constructed have since been removed for
building materials, and the mound itself is now reduced in size year
by year by the operation of the plough." Near this Tumulus,
which is also described as of oval form, is found a few hundred
yards to the South another of circular shape. This was opened in
1869 by Mr. G. F. Playne, assisted by Mr. A. E. Smith, of
Nailsworth, and is thus described. "The materials forming the
central portion of the mound were removed down to the original
surface of the ground. The upper portion was found to consist of
stone and rubble to the depth of 18 inches, the remaining 3 feet 6
inches was fine mould. In this fine mould 80 flints were found, also
4 small pieces of pottery, and a few teeth of oxen. On what had
been the surface soil before the construction of the barrow, traces
of the action of fire were perceptible; charcoal, burned bones, and
small pieces of a human scull lay scattered about, whilst exactly at
the centre of the tumulus a hole eight inches in depth had been
made, and in it lay a few burned human bones. The flints were found
in every part of the heap of fine mould; some were flaked thin, and
sharp edged, forming scraping or cutting implements......One flint

CHAVENAGE

arrow-point, of uncommon type, lay near the deposited bones. No trace of metal was observed. The pottery, rude in structure, was ornamented by a pattern formed by dotted lines."

THE CHURCHYARD FIELD.

We continue along the road to Chavenage and very soon descend into a valley known as Ledgemore Bottom. The road for a little distance is flanked by woods on either hand, and as soon as we pass them we come to what has been called from time immemorial "The Churchyard Field." Dudley Fosbrook says, "there is a tradition that a Church once stood there, but without any support from record or excavation. I apprehend certain yew trees adjacent furnished the denomination." This account by Dudley Fosbrook, who was Curate-in-charge of Horsley at the close of the last century bears witness at any rate to the great age of the yew trees which still exist, for they must have appeared even a century ago of very ancient date to have been considered the origin of a tradition that a Church once stood there. A Clergyman who visited some ancient yew trees on an island in Loch Lomond this last summer, and which were being examined at the time by some learned society who declared many of the trees to be 1500 years old, gives it as his opinion that the yews in the Churchyard Field are of the same age. The largest of these yews at six feet from the base measures twenty-three feet. If a church or churchyard formerly existed there it must have been in Saxon or British times. No human remains have been found in this field, but an old man still living says, that some forty years ago, when ploughing the field, he ploughed up a stone with an inscription on it, and that it looked like a grave stone. The stone was buried again. The field has just lately been ploughed by the steam cultivator, but no remains were discovered. Only a very much worn silver coin was picked up, so much worn that nothing can be told about it. And it may be mentioned, that one whose word may be relied on declares, that years back he came by accident upon a stone, which he took for a grave stone in the adjoining copse. Search has been made for this since but it cannot be found. It is not unlikely that in early times a hamlet or village existed hereabout, for it is a sheltered nook with good water close by, and it is in the vicinity of two ancient roads, one passing each end of the field.[1] Further on these two roads converge into one as they approach Chavenage Green.

---

[1] Dudley Fosbrook speaks of one Will Osborne, who died, seized of a toft called Luddesmore, in Horsley, and two parcels of pasture, and a close of meadow of

BRITISH AND SAXON GRAVES AT CHAVENAGE.

Here too, ancient burying places are found. Two circular tumuli were opened in a field near Chavenage in 1847, from which were obtained iron spearheads, bronze fibulæ, silver earrings, stone, clay, and amber beads: all characteristic specimens of Anglo-Saxon workmanship. On the same spot a further search was made by Mr. Playne in 1870, who, digging below these Anglo-Saxon graves, came upon others of earlier date, which contained, like the Lechmore Tumuli, charcoal, burned bones, small pieces of pottery, worked flint, and a well worked flint javelin point.

The tumuli found in Hazlewood, as already mentioned, are said to be of the same ancient character as these last, and others like them have been opened in Horsley Wood.

SAXON RECORDS.

There is interesting mention of the surrounding district in a contemporary record of a Mercian Witan, held at Gloucester in 896, and which is published in Dr. Pauli's Life of Alfred. The Witan was summoned by Ethelred, son-in-law of Alfred, the bishops and nobles attending.

Werfrith, the Bishop of Worcester, in which diocese Gloucester-shire, East of the Severn was then included, addressed the Witan, and declared "that all the forest land which belonged to Wuduceastre (Woodchester), and the usufruct of which was formerly given for ever by King Ethelbald at Worcester to Bishop Werfrith as drift and cutting, had been taken possession of, and said that it had been taken partly at Bislege (Bisley), partly at Aveningas (Avening), partly at Scorranstane (Cherrington ?) and partly at Thornbyrig (Thornbury), as he believed. Then all the Witan answered that right must be done to the Church as well as everyone else." Noble sentiments! Would that modern Parliaments might give heed to it! Then the offending noble Athelwald expressed his desire to do right, and to allow "every Church its share." And he "ordered his vassal Eglaf to ride thither with Wulfhun and the priest of the place, and he made him draw out all the boundaries as he read them in the old books, and as King Ethelbald had formerly marked them when he made a present of the land." Only Athelwald wished the right of hunting to be reserved to him at

eight acres, and thirty acres of arable in the Conygre Field, and three half-acres held of the King. The King was King Charles, but whether Charles I. or II. does not appear There are two cottages at Ledgemore at the present time, but it is a lonely spot. Whether these cottages indicate the existence of other dwellings in former days I know not,

Langanhrycge, (the Ridge?) "And so the priest of the place and
Athelwald's vassal rode through the land, first to Guinethlaege,
and Roddunbeorg (Rodborough) itself, then to Smececumb and
Sengetlege, then to Heardenlege, that is also called Dryganlege,
(Dursley?) as far as Little Naegleslege (Nailsworth?) and Athelferth's land. Thus Athelwald's man showed him the boundaries
as the old books fix and prove them."

As the forest land of Woodchester was in dispute, and that of
Avening, it is not unlikely that the Naegleslege referred to was
Nailsworth. And in defining these disputed boundaries, the
boundary of the Manor of Horsley would in part be traversed.
The record also bears witness to the forest-like character of the
district.

The Athelferth referred to might be Ethelbert, Alfred's second
brother. His eldest brother, Ethelbald, gave the forest land of
Woodchester to the Church, not as King, I suppose, but as a
private individual giving his own property.

If, therefore, Woodchester and Avening belonged to Ethelbald,
Horsley might have been the property of Ethelbert his brother.
At all events history may corroborate this conjecture, for in the
days of Edward the Confessor, the Manor of Horsley was then a
Royal domain.

HORSLEY AT THE NORMAN CONQUEST.

According to Domesday Book, the Manor had belonged to Goda,
the sister of Edward the Confessor.[1]

After the Conquest it was given by William the Conqueror to
Roger de Montgomery, Earl of Shrewsbury, who in turn presented
it to the Abbey of St. Martin, which he had lately founded at
Troarn, in Normandy. Before the compilation of the Domesday
Book (1084), a Prior and a few Monks from Troarn had settled in
the parish and established a cell, and the Manor of Horsley
remained the property of these Norman Monks for nearly three
centuries.

---

[1] EXTRACT FROM "DOMESDAY BOOK."
Kindly obtained for me by Thomas Hallowes, Esq., of Tavistock Square.
Glowecscire.

xxiii. Terra Æcclæ. De Troarz. In Langetrew Hd.

Eccla. S. Martini de Troarz ten. Horselei dono regis. W. Goda
tenuit soror. R. E. Ibi x. hidæ. In Dnio. sunt iiii. car. 7 vi.
villi. 7 v. bord. cu. v. car. 7 un. Radchenist. 7 in Glouuecestre | de una Domus
vi. den, Ibi molin. de L. denar, Valuit. xii. lib. modo. xiiii. lib,

In the reign of Edward III., and about the year 1372, the Manor of Horsley passed into the hands of the Prior and Convent of Bruton, in the County of Somerset. It appears that the Prior of Bruton had lands at a place called Lyon, in Normandy, which he gave to the Abbey of Troarn in exchange for the Manors of Horsley and Whitminster. But a few years later, in the fifth year of King Richard II., the Abbey of Bruton was disseized (dispossessed) of the Manor of Horsley, because it withdrew from the maintenance of six poor persons and a Prior and Canon to pray for the souls of William the Conqueror and his successors, and one John Serle and others were put in possession. It is plain from this that the Prior of Bruton, on acquiring his new property, was not careful to fulfil the original conditions imposed upon it by Roger de Montgomery. The exchange had been made with the sanction of the Bishop, for Bigland says in his History of Gloucestershire—"The tythes of the parish of Horsley were appropriated by Henry Wakefield, Bishop of Worcester, in 1376, to the Abbey of Bruton ; " but when the Abbey of Bruton withdrew from its responsibility it is evident the Bishop interfered to see that justice was done. This I believe to have been the reason why the Abbey of Bruton was disseized of the Manor, but it was soon restored. It is recorded that it was restored in the same year, viz., the fifth of King Richard II., or 1382. If instead of the fifth of King Richard II. we might read the third, and a mistake might easily be made in transcribing a number, this would further accord with what is told us by Bigland, who goes on to say, "In 1380, he—the Bishop —appointed twelve marks to be paid annually to the officiating priest which stipend has not been increased." This statement is also supported by a letter sent by the Tithe Commissioners to a former Vicar of Horsley in 1872, which says, "It would appear that the Vicarage of this parish was endowed by an ordinance (the original of which is in the Registry at Worcester, in which diocese the parish then was), made in 1380 by the Bishop of Worcester, by which he decreed and ordained the Vicar to be settled to the Church of Horsley, and to receive of the Prior and Convent of Bruton (who were then the owners of the Impropriate Rectory) in the name of his portion of the Vicarage aforesaid, twelve marks sterling in money, counted at two parts of the year, viz. :—at the Feast of St. Michael and the Nativity of St. John the Baptist, by equal portions, and four cartloads of wood or fuel, by deliverance of the Keeper of the wood of the said Priory and Convent, at the end of four usual parts of the year. These 12 marks (£8) have been from that time paid by

BRUTON CHURCH.

the Impropriate Rector to the Vicar, and in lieu of the four cart-loads of wood, the owner of the Wood (now called Horsley Wood) has immemorially paid the Vicar £2 2s. a year.''

It is an interesting fact that this endowment of £8 a year, which was in the first place assigned by the Earl of Shrewsbury in the days of King William I. as the stipend of the Vicar of Horsley— *i.e.* the deputy of the various Abbots to whom the Manor belonged —and which was recovered and secured to the succeeding Vicars by the action of the Bishop of the diocese in the year 1380, is still received. It is an interesting fact that a presbyter of the same Church, after the lapse of 800 years receives the same. It is also an interesting fact that one of the main conditions on which this Endowment was given, we are still able to fulfil. We do not indeed pray for the souls of the departed, but can still pray and do pray for the souls of William the Conqueror's successors, in that we pray publicly and privately for his descendants—Victoria our Queen, the Prince of Wales, and all the members of the Royal Family. These facts say much for the love of justice which has generally prevailed in our Nation, and for the stability of our National Institutions; and we heartily pray that they may long continue. The two guineas a year, in lieu of the four cartloads of wood, is still paid annually out of the estate of Col. Kingscote. If after a right and title of 800 years the Church should be deprived of these payments, it would be barefaced robbery and sacrilege.

The Abbey of Bruton retained possession of the Manor of Horsley until the dissolution of the Monastries in the days of Henry VIII.

As the Priors or Abbots of Bruton were, by virtue of their office, lords of the Manor of Horsley for a space of 170 years, I give a list of their names, as kindly furnished me by the present Vicar of Bruton. It will however be seen that the list is by no means complete.

PRIORS AND ABBOTS OF BRUTON.

A. D. 1416—John, was summoned to Convocation.

,, 1418—John Corsham, Prior, died 10th December.

,, 1429—John Schoyle, resigned.

,, 1429—8th August — Richard Glastonbury; he died 14th September, 1448.

,, 1488—4th October—John Henton. There were fourteen Canons in the Convent, and two were absent, having renounced their profession. John Henton was summoned to Convocation, 30th June, 1463.

A. D. 1498—William Gilbert was Prior. He was Suffragan Bishop
to Cardinal Wolsey, when he held the bishopric of
Bath and Wells, in commendam with the title Epis-
copus Majorensis; he was instituted into the Vicarage
of South Petherton, 16th December, 1525. Leland
says he went to Rome and obtained a grant from the
Pope to change the style of this Convent from Priory
to Abbey.

,, 1553? (or 1533)—John Ely was Abbot. He and fourteen
Monks surrendered the Abbey, April 1st, 1539. He
had a yearly pension of £80, and a gratuity of £20.

THE NAME GLASTONBURY.

There seems one name in the above list of special local interest.
Glastonbury is a name which recurs very frequently in our Registers,
from the time of Queen Elizabeth downwards One has often
wondered what brought a name, evidently of Somersetshire origin,
into the place, and I have observed that the Glastonburys always
have been fond of the name Richard. There was a Richard
Glastonbury, resident in Horsley, in the days of Queen Elizabeth,
and there is a Richard Glastonbury still living in the parish. And
a Richard Glastonbury was Lord of the Manor of Horsley and Prior
of Bruton, in the middle of the 15th Century. It would be a
slander on the fair fame of the holy Prior to suggest that the
present Glastonburys are his descendants, but not unlikely some
younger or poorer branch of his family were settled here, and
perhaps gratitude to their benefactor caused the family to enter-
tain a traditional affection for the name Richard.

THE BARTON AT BARTON END.

"At Barton End," says Bigland, "was the Barton for storing the
corn rents belonging to the Abbey of Bruton . . . . Certain
Manorial privileges are claimed by this tything." What the
privileges were Bigland does not say. Plainly this Barton gave the
name 'Barton End.' It's a warning to all against readily deter-
mining derivations to read what the late Sidney Dobell thought about
it. In his "Life and Letters," we are told he was interested in the
name of his house, and wrote to a friend: "Barton is evidently either
Bardon, the bard's hill, or *Baldon*, the hill of Apollo (Bel or Baal).
I incline to the last derivation." One wonders he should have gone
so far away in search of a derivation, when the obvious one was
so near.

Horsley was anciently divided into four tithings, and until four years ago each tithing was rated separately. They were Barton End, Nup End, Tickmor End, and Nailsworth.

DISSOLUTION OF THE ABBEY.

In the year 1536 an Act was passed for the dissolution of the smaller Monasteries, and in 1539, another, for legalizing the dissolution of other Monasteries, and granting them to the King. This later Act probably sealed the doom of the Abbey of Bruton, for as already stated, it was on April 1st, 1539, that John Ely and fourteen monks surrendered the Abbey, and with it all its belongings would fall to the King. The Manor of Horsley now became the property of Henry VIII.

HORSLEY MANOR THE PROPERTY OF THE CROWN.

Three years later, in 1542, the Manor of Horsley, with lands called "Crainmere," were granted by the King to Sir Thomas Seymour, the brother of the King's late wife, Jane Seymour, and uncle to King Edward VI. He was afterward created Earl of Hertford and Duke of Somerset, and on the death of King Henry, he obtained for himself the chief authority in the Kingdom, under the title of Lord Protector. He was the firm and zealous patron of those who promoted the Reformation, but he gained far too great a portion of Church property, to be deemed disinterested in the share which he had in the destruction of the Monasteries. He appropriated Church property to the erection of a new palace for himself, described as a vast and splendid pile, and which bequeathed its name to the building now on the same site, Somerset House, in the Strand. He incurred the hatred of the Duke of Northumberland, who eventually encompassed his fall. He was arrested on a charge of treason, and was executed on Tower hill, January 20th, 1552.

OF SIR WALTER DENNYS.

On the attainder and death of Somerset, the Manor of Horsley was granted to Sir Walter Dennys, or Dennis, of Dyrham, in this county. This Sir Walter Dennis seems to have had some former connection with the parish, for Rudder mentioned that he was seized of lands in Horsley and Thevenage (Chavenage), in the 28th year of Henry VIII., which would be the year 1537.

OF THE STEPHENS FAMILY.

The son of Sir Walter next sold the Manor to the family of

Stephens, of Eastington.[1]   Richard Stephens, Esq., in the reign of
Queen Elizabeth, built the present Mansion at Chavenage,[2] in 1576,
and settled the "Chavenydge Farm." on his wife Anne, one of the
daughters of John Stone, haberdasher, of London, in 1589.   The
house is built with two wings, and a central projection for a porch
and entrance hall, so that the ground plan represents the letter E.
Rudder says, writing in 1779, "The Manor and Estate have continued
ever since in the same name and family.   The Rev. Mr. Robert
Stephens, of Chavenage, being the present proprietor of them."
Many monuments belonging to the Stephens' family are to be found
in Eastington Church, and a portion of the old Court House at
Eastington, which was also their property, is still standing
between the Churchyard and the high road.   The Manor of Horsley
is still the property of the descendants of the Stephenses, though
the present owner and lady of the Manor is named Cave.

THE RECTORY AND TITHES.

Previous to the Dissolution of the Monasteries, the Abbot of
Bruton was both Lord of the Manor and Rector.   The Vicar was
his deputy in Ecclesiastical or Spiritual things, and had the pay of
a deputy.   The Manor was bestowed, as before stated, by Henry
VIII., on his brother-in-law, Sir Thomas Seymour; but the
Rectory and tithes were retained by the Crown until the sixth year of
Queen Elizabeth.   In 1564, Elizabeth granted them to Sir Walter
Hungerford, Knight of Farley Castle, Wiltshire.   They were held
successively by families of the name of Willett, Hillier, Selfe,
and Leversage.   The following note by the hand of Dudley
Fosbrook, says:
    "1797: The great tithes came by the decease of a Mr. Hillier
(vide Burials, 1797,) into the possession of John Selfe, Esq., by
purchase of the reversionary right; they had before belonged to
Leversage, who married a Miss Hillier, to whom they had been
bequeathed.   During the life of the aforesaid Mr. Hillier, they
were held by a Mr. Leversage, son of the above Leversage and
Hillier."   Then follows a correction of this note.   "This is one
information: According to Mr. Willbraham, they were given by
marriage of a daughter as a part of the dowry to the Selfe family,

---

1 Fosbrook remarks that " when the Manor was sold to the family of Stephens,
there were sold also immense parcels upon lease for 1000 years, including
extensive common rights, which by various surreptitious inclosures are reduced
to nothing."

2 The derivation of Chavenage is probably Avon-Edge

who disposed of them for three lives to the Leversages, after the expiration of whose interests they came again to the above John Selfe, Esq., and after his death (1800), to his brother Richard Selfe." Another note made in the same year says: " Oct. and Nov. 1797. The great tithes offered for sale in parcels by the impropriator, and bought in part by various persons."

Some portion of this tithe, described on the deed, " The Rectory," was, in 1810, purchased by Robert Kingscote for £3,000. This was retained by the Kingscote family until the year 1855, when it was given up by Col. T. Kingscote on the payment of £1,500 by the late Miss Bathurst, who was then resident at Barton End House, and this lady presented it to the Vicar for the augmentation of the living. The yearly value of this tithe is about £80.

But the tithe must originally have produced a large sum. By the tithe terrier, made in 1841, the tithe on upwards of 3,300 acres, is declared merged and extinguished on the freehold. There was still a portion of tithe payable to Thomas Shewell Bailward, Esq., and others, on some 127 acres producing a sum of £31 3s. 3d. a year; but this was by deed merged in the freehold in 1851. The tithe still left, and which is now paid to the Vicar, arises from about 310 acres, and produces £80. Therefore we may reckon that as the parish contains upwards of 4,000 acres, the whole of the tithe, if it had remained, would now have been worth about £1,000 a year.

The Alienation of Tithe a grievous wrong to the Church.

This wholesale spoliation of Ecclesiastical property evidently caused great injury to the parish. My opinion is, the parish has not recovered the loss yet. The Monks, who were doubtless the teachers (according to their light) and almoners to the people were taken away. The maintenance of six poor persons, which they were also bound to by the condition on which they held the Manor, was no more thought of when the Manor went to the King. And the Manor, a century ago, was worth £2000 a year. Yet out of such spoils the King thought it sufficient to leave the Vicar, now doubtless also turned out of home, with the miserable pittance of £8 a year, and his yearly four cartloads of wood. Some people say the State endowed the Church, but here is a case (and it was not alone) of an opposite character:—the Church and people were robbed, and they, to whom the Crown afterwards granted the spoils, were consenting parties. Very bold and faithful was the language of

Archbishop Whitgift addressed to Queen Elizabeth on this matter. His expostulation is found in the Life of Richard Hooker. He says, "I beg posterity to take notice of what is already become visible in many families; that Church land, added to an ancient and just inheritance, hath proved like a moth fretting a garment, and secretly consumed both: or like the eagle that stole a coal from the altar, and thereby set her nest on fire, which consumed both her young eagles and herself that stole it." "And though I should forbear to speak reproachfully of your father; yet I beg you to take notice, that a part of the Church's rights, added to the vast treasure left him by his father, hath been conceived to bring an unavoidable consumption upon both, notwithstanding all his diligence to preserve them." And after he says, "Madam, religion is the foundation and cement of human societies! and when they that serve at God's Altar shall be exposed to poverty, then religion itself will be exposed to scorn, and become contemptible; as you may already observe it to be in too many poor Vicarages in this nation."

HORSLEY UNCARED FOR.

For more than two centuries Horsley was left practically uncared for. The Vicar could hardly be called 'passing rich' on £8 a year. The marvel is that anyone was found to take the office. The Reformation was indeed a blessing, but should not have been accompanied by robbery. When the Horsley Priory was dissolved, the endowments should have been devoted to the increase of the Minister's Stipend, and the building and endowment of Schools. As it was, no wonder the inhabitants of Horsley, in the middle of the last century, were described as wicked and idle, and addicted to vicious habits, and as a consequence, also miserably poor. And where such habits get a hold on a secluded and unchangeable population, it takes generations to eradicate them.

EXONERATED FROM PAYMENT OF FIRST FRUITS.

The following document seems cruel irony when we consider the poverty in which Horsley was left. "These are to certify, that in a certain record remaining in the custody of the Remembrancer of First Fruits and Tenths, in the Exchequer of our Lord the King, at Westminster, containing the true yearly value of divers Ecclesiatical benefices in the County of Gloucester, according to a valuation made in pursuance of an Act of Parliament, 26th, Henry VIII., there is contained as follows:

VIEW FROM LANE LEADING TO HARTLEY BRIDGE.

STONEHOUSE DECANAL.

"Horseley Vicar, per ann Clare valet, £vij. xjs. iiijd.
xth inde xvs. id. obq.

The above Vicarage is exonerated from the payment of First Fruits and Tenths.

THOS. NEWSOM,
Deputy Remembrancer."

These First Fruits and Tenths, prior to the Reformation, were paid to the Pope, but were appropriated by Henry VIII., and remained the property of the Crown, until Queen Anne restored them to the Church by creating the Queen Anne's Bounty board to receive them and apply them to the augmentation of poor livings. Most of our old parishes still pay these First Fruits, and the Queen Anne's Bounty is yearly applying the income thus derived to the benefit of poor livings. Horsley having afforded the King pretty good plunder, was exonerated from the payment of this tax.

THE PRIORY.

Of course the first thing the Norman Monks would do on coming to take possession of their newly acquired inheritance, would be to choose a suitable site for their Church and Monastery. In so large a manor, many sites might have been found, but I have no doubt they were guided in their choice, not only by the beauty of the prospect which still surrounds the place where the old Priory stood, but also by reason of its close proximity to the junction of three ancient ways.

The Priory stood on the site, or very nearly on the site, of the recent prison. There is no description of it in any of the Histories of Gloucestershire, except a few bare notices of the existence of its ruins at the close of the last century. Thus Rudder, in 1779, writes: "The Prior of Bruton had a seat here, of which little more than the gateway remains. There was also, near the Church, a building called the chapel, now reduced to ruins." Bigland also says (1786): "Still to be discovered are the foundations of a considerable building, and the old gateway remains entire, standing near the Church." Dudley Fosbrook incidentally remarks that "the Prior's cell was but lately demolished, to form part of the Chapel at Chavenage House." There can be no doubt that most of the ruins were cleared away to make room for the prison. Some portion of these ruins are apparently built into the cottage at the corner of the Churchyard, and known as Ivy House; and a portion of a column, once belonging to it, may be seen at Nailsworth,

C

where it now forms part of Mr. Tabram's office. According to a statement contained in a work by Wedlake and Brayley, and published in 1810; "The painted windows of the Priory were built up in the house at Chavenage." In the large hall of Chavenage House these windows may still be seen; they consist chiefly of coats-of-arms or parts of coats-of-arms, in some cases put together upside down, and scraps of plain white glass are inserted in all directions to fill up gaps. Three white figures at the top, of very Ecclesiastical appearance, seem to be those of Saints or Monks, but as there is no sign of a nimbus they are probably intended for the latter, and represent perhaps Priors of Horsley, or Abbots of Bruton.

ITS FISHPONDS.

Below the hill, on which the Priory stood, were the fishponds belonging to it. The field to the right of Hartley Bridge, through which the footpath to Hazlecote passes, is still called by the native folk "The Fishers." A very cursory examination will convince anyone the field was once a pond, and the remains of the weir and dam may still be seen at the neck of the valley, where it approaches Hartley Bridge. The field below Hartley Bridge was evidently also a pond. Another pond, in which parish tradition says the Monks "kept their fish," is to be seen in the field beyond the Churchyard.

There was a picture in the Exhibition of the Royal Academy of 1880, entitled "Preparing for Friday," which was like what must often have been seen in the olden time at Horsley. A party of Monks were represented as engaged in fishing, and on the high ground in the distance stood the Monastery and village, to which they belonged.

THE PRISON.

At the close of the last century the site of the Ancient Priory was covered by the prison. Bigland says, "Pursuant to an Act of Parliament, passed in 1783, a Penitentiary and House of Correction have been lately completed at Horsley, upon land given by Henry Stephens, Esq., for the adjoining hundreds. This plan is particularly judicious, and calculated to answer every purpose of a reformed police." It was one of the four County Prisons, the others being respectively at Little Dean, North Leach, and Lawford's Gate. Four years ago the Horsley Prison was closed, sold, pulled down, and converted into a "New Mansion." It is to be hoped the present owner will call it "The Priory," which certainly sounds better, and might commemorate the fact, that on the same site the Ancient Priory of Horsley stood for the space, including the time when it was a ruin, of more than 700 years.

THE CHURCH.

It is doubtful whether there was any Church within the limits of the parish of Horsley before the Norman Conquest. If there was one in more primitive times in the vicinity of the so called "Churchyard Field" at Ledgemore, it must have been in British times. There is no reference to a Church as formerly existing, when the Domesday Book was compiled. The present Church is dedicated to St. Martin. The Manor, as before noticed, was given by Roger Montgomery, Earl of Shrewsbury, to the Abbey of St. Martin at Troarn, therefore, the inference is, there was no Church at Horsley before that time, because the dedication is to St. Martin; and for the same reason that the Church was founded while Horsley was still the property of the Norman Abbey of St. Martin. The French, in ancient times, had such an esteem for the memory of St. Martin, that it is said they carried his helmet with them into their wars, as an ensign to encourage them to bravery. And their fondness for him is also shown by the fact, that after their conquest of our own land, they dedicated so many Churches to his memory. He was formerly a soldier and then a Bishop, and was made Bishop of Tours, A.D. 374. By his earnest preaching, he everywhere persuaded many of the Gauls to renounce their idolatry, and embrace Christ; whilst he destroyed their idol temples and broke down their images. He obtained the title of the Apostle of the Gauls.

The parish Church being dedicated to his memory, I take as a proof that the first Church was built whilst the Norman Monks were in possession, and I would date its building soon after their arrival.

The Church, which was pulled down about 44 years ago, seems to have been built when the Abbey of Bruton came into possession, about 300 years after the Conquest. Bigland says, "The Church was probably re-built by the Abbey of Bruton in the Middle Centuries." The Abbey of Bruton came into possession, as we know, in the year 1372; so this fact fixes the date of the second Church. It could not have been earlier than the 14th century, and the style of architecture corroborates this assertion. To the same date belongs the present Tower. The Vicar of Bruton has kindly sent me a photograph of Bruton Parish Church, which, while it has a splendid West Tower, has also a Tower over the North Porch; very curiously resembling the Tower of Horsley. This 14th century Church many old inhabitants remember, and it is described by Rudder. It is said to have been large, with an aisle on the South side, and a small aisle on the North side, called St. George's Chapel. A sketch of that old Church is here given. It is from a painting, executed I believe, by one of the Misses Young, daughter of Admiral Young, a former occupant of Barton End House. One other very good picture of the old Church is in the possession of Mr. W. Axen.

The chief entrance to the old Church was on the South side—*i. e.* on the side towards the Priory; while the chief entrance to the present Church is on the North, towards the village.

The present Church was built in 1838, at a cost of £3,800, which was raised by public subscription, the names of the subscribers being recorded by a tablet in the vestry.

During the past year the gallery at the West end of the Church has been removed, and the partition wall, which filled up the ancient Arch, thus dividing the body of the Church from the Tower, was taken down, and now the Tower is made open to the Church. The expense was generously borne by Major Williams. During the progress of the work, the middle floor of the Tower, consisting of solid oak beams of great thickness (probably as old as the Tower), was found to be so rotten that it had to be taken down, and a new floor was put in by subscription. It was proposed also that a penny subscription should be started for a new window for the Tower, the old mullions being 18th century work, and hideously ugly. So successful has been this appeal, that during the past year we have collected about £40, and new mullions and tracery in keeping with the ancient architecture of the tower, have been executed and built in, and it is proposed to complete the window, when sufficient funds are available, by filling it with stained glass, to illustrate the life of St. Martin, to whose memory the Church is dedicated.

The pair of oak candlesticks, standing on the communion table, were turned by Major Williams out of a portion of the Nailsworth Peace Pole. This pole was erected at Nailsworth, to commemorate the Peace of 1815. It was cut out of a remarkable straight oak, which grew at Shortwood, and which an old Nailsworth inhabitant says, was one of the sights of its day. After serving as the Peace Pole for some 60 years, it was blown down; then cut into portions, and one portion was made into the above-named candlesticks.

THE CHURCH BELLS.

We have a peal of six. They appear to have been given in the days of King Charles I., for two still retain the date; the others

ST. MARTIN'S, HORSLEY,
BEFORE THE YEAR
1839.

appear to have been recast since. There is an inscription on each
as follows:

2nd Bell, "Anno Domini, 1632. I B T M."

3rd Bell, "Anno Domini, 1632. I B T M."

4th Bell, "Cast at Gloucester by John Rudhall, 1796."

5th Bell, "Mears and Stainbank, London, 1871." (This is said
to have cost £60 for recasting.)

Tenor Bell, "John Harvey and William Griffiths, Churchwardens, Mr. Richard Davies, Vicar, 1776." (A Memorandum in parish books, dated 1775, records that "the tenor
bell which was broken was recast at Gloucester."

Treble Bell, "Peace and good neighbourhood. A. R. 1712."

THE CHURCHYARD.

The following information, gathered from the copy of a deed
executed in the year 1812, may be of interest. It seems that
originally the Churchyard was "small and confined," and at the
beginning of this century was deemed insufficient for a burial
ground for this parish. Then a piece of ground, containing half-
an-acre or thereabout, was laid on to the Churchyard, but was
distinguished therefrom for some years by landmarks set and
affixed within the surface of the ground. In 1812, this piece of
ground, which belonged to Admiral James Young, of Barton End
House, was, by the deed above mentioned, made over to the Vicar
and Churchwardens for the time being, to be used as part of the
Churchyard, on condition that Admiral Young should no longer be
considered liable to the repairs of the Chancel, or to certain
payments called Procurations and Synodals. One wonders how
Admiral Young became legally responsible for the repairs of the
Chancel, but I suspect he was the owner of some portion of the
Rectorial tithe, on which this charge was made.

At the end of the above named deed is the following note:

"1823, July 21st.—The following entry appears in the Minute
Book of the Vestry Meeting of the Parish of Horsley:—'At a
regular Vestry Meeting, held this day, an application was made by
the trustees of the Charity School, after notice given in the Church,
for permission to erect a new School building in some part of the
unconsecrated ground in the Churchyard, to which we agree,
considering it to be for the benefit of the parish.'" Signed by Vicar
and others present.

This was an illegal proceeding, and I am sorry to say was not the
last of which the Horsley Vestry has been guilty, even with the

Vicar in the chair. The land was given for the purpose of a graveyard, and the Vicar and Churchwardens and others were simply the Trustees; it was not in their power to appropriate any part of their trust to another and different purpose. The wrong doing brought its trouble, for when in 1855 it was found necessary to make some alterations in the School and to seek help from the Committee of Council on Education, it was found the Trustees had no title. A long correspondence between the then Vicar and the Committee of Council ensued. The lawyers were perplexed—their Lordships' learned counsel expressed "much difficulty in advising upon the case," but at length, after much labour and expense, and the bothering of many people, the title was made good. The moral is, "Beware of doing illegal things." In 1823, the School was built on the illegally acquired site, it being part of the uncon-secrated ground of the Churchyard. And no part of the uncon-secrated ground was used for burial until the year 1839, when the remainder was consecrated by the Bishop of the diocese, and the hereinbefore abstracted indenture of the 27th November, 1812, was then handed to the Bishop's Secretary, and is now in the Registry at Gloucester.

Now observe how the above transaction has resulted. A lay Rector was released from his liability; his estate escaped the charge once laid upon it to repair a considerable portion of the Church. The Ratepayers accepted the liability, which was never fulfilled by them, and it cannot be enforced now, because of the Church Rate Abolition Act. The land was given by a Churchman for Church purposes, but by a recent Act, (Burials Amendment Act,) it may be used up by other communities without any charge, or any provision for another graveyard for Church people. This graveyard is now full, in fact what was the new ground seems to have been used in ancient times for burials, for on looking into a newly dug grave one day, I observed to the Sexton he had come down to a hard rock, when he removed a stone and said, no, he had come to an ancient grave. It belonged to a time when they buried without coffins, the body had been laid in the ground, and large stones had been care-fully placed over it, to support the superincumbent earth.

THE VICARAGE.

Before the Reformation, I suppose the Vicars resided with the Monks at the Priory adjoining the Church. Later, a Vicarage seems to have been acquired, which stood somewhere opposite the Bell Inn, at Horsley. This old Vicarage is referred to in a terrier

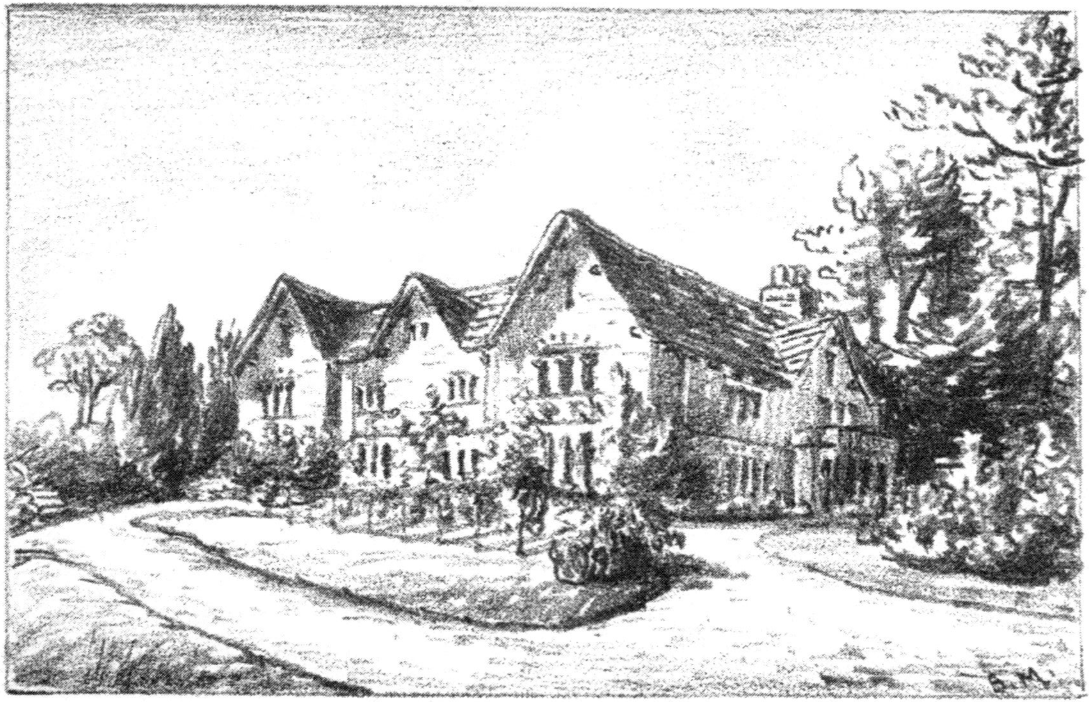

HORSLEY VICARAGE.

drawn up by the Vicar and some of the principal inhabitants by order of the Bishop in the year 1807.

"Item. The Land Tax of the Vicarage of Horsley was redeemed in the year 1799 with money procured by the sale of the *old Vicarage House and garden*. The surplus money, after the redemption of the Land Tax was vested in the three per cents reduced Stocks, and now stands there in the name of Edward Wilbraham, Esq., of the parish of Horsley, as trustee for the existing Vicar of Horsley, and produces an annual dividend of four pounds, seven shillings, and eightpence." To this day this amount is paid to the Vicar by the Solicitors of the late Mr. Wilbraham.

The old Vicarage, known as Rockness, was purchased about the middle of the last century. At or about the same time the adjoining glebe was bought. The purchase money was found partly by Mr. Peter Castleman, aided by a grant from Queen Anne's Bounty. The Rockness House will always be of interest as the place where the Rev. Dudley Fosbrook wrote his History of Gloucestershire. This Vicarage was sold in 1878 by Rev. J. H. Shaw,—after having obtained the requisite permission from the Bishop of the Diocese and the Archbishop of Canterbury—because it was a continual burden on so small a living in consequence of the heavy dilapidations so constantly recurring. The money was placed in the keeping of the Queen Anne's Bounty, and yields a yearly interest of £9.

The present Vicarage was built about 34 years ago by the Rev. E. N. Mangin, on a portion of the glebe. The site is described in old documents as "The Grove Ground and Woodland." The house is prettily and substantially built, and with its surroundings commanding as it also does a lovely prospect, can hardly be matched in the County of Gloucester.

THE VICARS.

A list of Vicars with their patrons from the Reformation to the present time. The list is as accurate as I can make it. My sources of information are chiefly the Histories of Gloucestershire, the Monuments in the Church, and the Registers.

Vicars.	Patrons.
1554 Thomas Wodehouse	Thomas Bennett, by grant from the Abbey of Bruton, dated 1536
1558 Richard Devys	Queen Elizabeth.
1608 Samuel Cradock, M.A.	King James I.
1635 Samuel Hieron	King Charles I.
1640 Richard Horton	,,

1659 Nathaniel Hall, (married
    2nd wife, 1665)   Patron not known.
    Richard Stubbs, (died 1678, he was a Puritan Minister).
1690   ,,   Collins   The Lord Chancellor.
1704 John Gyles   ,,
    Thomas Stratford, (died 1732,   ,,
    See Tablet)
1733 Richard Wallington, M.A.,   ,,
    (See Tablet)
1764 George Gwinnett   ,,
1779 Richard Davies   ,,
    (He became also Vicar of Tetbury)
1794   Dudley Fosbrook } were Curates
1811   Anthony Keck }
1825 Samuel Lloyd   Bishop of Glo'ster and Bristol.
1849 Edward N. Mangin   Dr. Monk.
1862 Vaughan S. Fox   Dr. Thompson.
1868 Nathaniel Cornford   Dr. Ellicott.
1874 John Hall Shaw   ,,
1878 Messing Rudkin   ,,

The year 1602 gives a decided change of handwriting in registers, as if a change of Vicar. So again in 1630.

The Crown of course succeeded to the patronage after the confiscation of the Abbey of Bruton. Atkins says, speaking of the time when Mr. Collins was Incumbent, that the patron was the Lord Chancellor. The patronage was transferred to the Bishop, possibly because at that time it was not worth having.

Rudder, in 1779, says the Lord Chancellor was patron. Fosbrook, who became Curate in 1794, says distinctly the Bishop was patron.

Some of the above Vicars require special mention.

1. SAMUEL HIERON. Dudley Fosbrook says, "Mr. Hieron was ejected from the Church in the Civil Wars, and was the author of some religious books." There are several entries in the parish registers of baptisms of children of this Samuel Hieron, which indicate that he was Vicar of the parish as early as 1635.

Some of the above facts were mentioned in our Parish Magazine, when Mr. Charles Playne, of Theescombe, sent a large octavo volume of more than 1300 pages of Sermons and Devotions, by one "Samuel Hieron," and asking whether the author was the Vicar of Horsley of that name.

The following notes, made from a preface to some of the sermons, by one Robert Hill, dated March 29th, 1620, show that the author of the sermons was not the Vicar of Horsley.

The writer says that Samuel Hieron was the son of a most worthy pastor, who had been persuaded to enter the ministry "by that true saint of God, Master Fox," evidently meaning the author of the "Book of Martyrs," and that he was the Vicar of Epping, in Essex. At Epping, therefore, we may suppose Samuel Hieron was born. "He was sent in due time to the King's Schoole neare Windsor, thence to King's Colledge in Cambridge, where he made such progresse in a few years, that at his first showing of himself in that colledge, hee preached with such approbation and applause that to mee, who heard him often in his young yeares, he seemed rather a bachelor in divinitie than a bachelor of arts, and rather a divine of forty, than four and twenty yeares of age; yea, he was so much admired that hee became of such note whilst he stayed in London, that many congregations, yea, and the Inns of Court greatly desired to enjoy his ministrie. But being by that most learned and worthy provost, Sir Henrie Sauil, called to a charge in the gift of Eaton Colledge, hee following that call did so demeane himself in that place till he dyed, that not only the people of Modburie in Devon, but many other places of that countie and countrie were much comforted by his paines in preaching."

Now it is evident from this Preface,—which was written in 1620, after Hieron's death, that the author of the sermons was not the Minister of Horsley, whose name occurs in the register for the year 1635, and at intervals as late as 1654.

But the Samuel Hieron, the Minister of Horsley, was probably the son of the above. The author of the sermons we have seen was a very popular and well-known man in his day. His sermons show that whilst he was a staunch Evangelical, he was also a strong Churchman, and a sincere believer in the divine right of kings. At the end of the volume of sermons are four "learned and godly" discourses entitled, "A Present for Cæsar." Some of the language in these sermons is very strong, as for example, "I am now come to the last branch of outward submission, which is matters of necessary supply. Kings places are high and their occasions great, and many things pertaine to the supportation of their state, which the subjects must yield or supply: and this is twofold either of men, persons, or of their goods. If Kings shall become to extorting and abuse their liberty to the pressing of the subjects, I find not in the Word of God any allowance at all to make rebellion; such things must be borne with patience."

It is significant that these sermons were printed in 1628-29 at the very time the petition "Bill of Rights" was being forced by the House of Commons on the unwilling King Charles I., the object of which was to defend the country from arbitrary taxation. The sermons, we may imagine, would be regarded with favour by the court party; and now that the author was dead, their gratitude would be exhibited towards the son. And here we are confronted by two other facts which seem to make for the theory, that Samuel Hieron, the minister of Horsley, was the son of the great preacher. The living of Horsley was at that time in the gift of Charles I., and Samuel Hieron, at Horsley, was evidently also a staunch Royalist, because Dudley Fosbrooke records "he was ejected from the Church in the Civil Wars."

Whether he was ejected from Horsley, or some other place, does not appear; but most likely before the civil war broke out, he was preferred to a more valuable living. Rudder says, " on what authority I know not that Richard Horton was Vicar in 1640, and the condition of the registers seems to indicate that after 1640 and for some years, in fact during the civil wars there was no minister at all at Horsley, therefore it would seem that Samuel Hieron had gone to some other living, whence he was afterwards ejected by the Puritan party when they came into power." The solitary baptism of another child in 1654 might have been at the time of a subsequent visit.

It is interesting to know that the descendants of the Hierons are still living in this neighbourhood. Mr. C. Playne says, " Samuel Hieron (the author of the sermons,) is supposed to have been a forefather of the Hierons, my father's bailiff."

2. RICHARD HORTON. I judge from the condition of the registers after 1640 that he never came to the parish. The civil war broke out in 1642, and the Lord of the Manor and Squire of the parish being a Parliamentarian, and the district generally being in sympathy with that party, he may have considered the position unsafe.

3. NATHANIEL HALL. From several entries in the parish registers he was evidently Vicar from 1659 to at least 1665. He must have been appointed during the later period of the Commonwealth, for the Restoration of the Monarchy was not until May 29th, 1660. He seems to have been a connection of the Halls, of Beverston. He was married twice at Horsley, and on the second occasion a Mr. Hall, of Beverston, was witness to the marriage. There was a Richard Hall, Rector of Beverston, from 1617 to 1638. Another Richard Hall, son of the former, was Rector from 1638 to 1684.

This second Richard Hall had a son, Nathaniel, born 1646, died 1672; but he of course could not have been the Vicar of Horsley. Perhaps the Nathaniel Hall, of Horsley, was brother to the second Richard Hall, of Beverston.

4. HENRY STUBBS, Puritan Preacher, seems to have followed Nathaniel Hall. Mr. Blunt in his list of Rectors of Dursley *(Dursley and its Neighbourhood)* after stating that the Rectory of Dursley was vacant from 1645 to 1660—the same was the case at Horsley—goes on to say, "Jos Woodward appears as minister for part of the time. Henry Stubbs was his assistant, and succeeded him. Stubbs was permitted to hold the benefice of Horsley, though not in holy orders until 1678, and dying in London in that year, was buried in Bunhill Fields. His Funeral Sermon was preached by his friend and unworthy fellow servant Richard Baxter, and is in print." Dudley Fosbrook supplies further information.—"Henry Stubbs, whose name is noted in the benefaction table of Horsley and Stinchcombe, was born at Bitton, entered Magdalen Hall, 1623, became B.A., 1627, and M.A., 1630. In the City of Wells he was one of the Commissioners for ejecting Scandalous Ministers, and afterwards became a preacher of considerable note at Dursley and this place; but ejecting himself by the Act of Conformity, he retired to London, and died in 1678. He wrote several divinity works."

In what year Henry Stubbs came to Horsley and how long he remained is not certain, but it must have been after the passing of the Act of Uniformity 1662. From 1665 to 1678, and after that date, very few entries of any kind occur in the register. If not in holy orders he was incurring great risk by preaching, and may not have cared to increase his danger by Baptising, Marrying, and Burying. He evidently found his position untenable, for Fosbrook says, "he ejected himself and retired to London." It is recorded by Rudder that the Rev. Henry Stubbs—time unknown—gave £20, vested in Mrs. Castleman, the interest to be laid out in purchasing testaments for the poor.

It is interesting to notice that Horsley has had two of its ministers ejected; we very often hear of the iniquity of the Act of Uniformity, whereby nearly 2000 Nonconforming Ministers were driven out of the Church—but judging from the example of Henry Stubbs, that law could not have been so very rigorously administered. While not in holy orders he appears to have been a preacher at Horsley after the passing of that Act and for some years. It is not fair to speak of the injustice of that Act, and not also to condemn the tyranny of the Puritans who ejected from 6000 to 8000 — the numbers are variously estimated — Episcopalian Clergymen from their cures during the Commonwealth. Hugh Robinson, who was Rector of Dursley from 1634—1645, was turned out by the Puritans and made to ride from Dursley to Gloucester with his face to the horse's tail.

What happened after the departure of Mr. Stubbs from Horsley, there is nothing to show. The Benefice was in the gift of King Charles II., but no appointment is recorded, and judging from the condition of the registers in the lack of regular entries, I should say things went on very badly in the parish until the reign of William and Mary, when Mr. Collins was made Vicar.

5. GEORGE GWINNELL, on resigning the Vicarage in 1776, was allowed a pension of £10 a year by the vestry for the rest of his life.

6. DUDLEY FOSBROOK, who says, "I was born in May 27th, 1770, was educated—1st, under a private tutor, a Clergyman at Billericay, afterwards at Petersfield, then at St. Paul's School; was elected scholar of Pembroke College, Oxford, in 1785, took the degree of B.A., and M.A., and in a worldly point of view, unhappily for myself, whose habits of application might have procured something like remuneration in another profession, was ordained Deacon upon the title of my scholarship in 1792, and settled in the curacy of this place, for which I was ordained Priest in 1794. He continued at Horsley until the year 1811, and during his residence at the old Vicarage, at Rockness, he wrote his History of Gloucestershire. His wife's relations, who are cottagers, are still living in the parish.

7. The REV. E. N. MANGIN was promoted by Dr. Baring, Bishop of Durham, to the Vicarage of Woodhorn with Newbiggin, in that diocese, where he died, 1879.

The following account of his funeral, which appeared in the "Stroud News," Oct 31st, 1879, bears testimony to his excellent worth.

"HORSLEY.—All who were privileged to know the beloved and highly revered former pastor of this parish, will be pleased to hear how highly he was esteemed and deeply mourned, not only by his parishioners generally, but by all classes and creeds for miles around. The extract is from the *Blyth Weekly News*, and is as follows:—

"'On Tuesday last, a large concourse of people of one accord met, from all points of the compass, at Woodhorn, many to attend the funeral, most to witness it; from Durham, and the distant parts of Northumberland, clergymen came to pay the last token of respect to "the good Vicar of Woodhorn" as he was designated. Never in the memory of man was such a sight witnessed here; the young and the old, both rich and poor, the native and the visitor, the near and the distant parishioner made it a point of duty to mark their respect to the worthy Vicar, and evince their sympathy for his bereaved and sorrowing family by their presence. Gentlemen left their desks and offices in Newcastle, and working men left their sphere of labour to travel to the scene of mourning. As the oak coffin, with its bright pall, was raised on loving shoulders, and borne from the door to the Church with reverend friends as pall-bearers, the family closely followed; then came the mourners clad in sombre black, without either scarfs or hatbands, and with uncovered heads, they marched sorrowfully along the carriage road, either side of which was lined with those waiting to fall into the ranks, the Church choirs of Woodhorn and Newbiggin following after the mourners. The coffin was carried into the chancel, accompanied by the family, pall bearers, and choir. The Church was densely crowded in every part, and the same feeling of awe, witnessed outside, was not more displayed by those who were seated inside. The burial service was conducted by the Curate of the parish, and the Vicar of Creswell. The choirs before leaving the Church sang the 317th hymn, and at the grave the 191st hymn. The coxswain, assistant-coxswain, and two of the crew of the life-boat, had the honour of bearing their beloved Secretary and revered pastor from the Chancel to the tomb. On the conclusion of the solemn service, after the family and mourners had taken 'their last fond look,' a way was opened up for all the assembled multitude (not less than 1,400) to pass the open grave, and take their farewell gaze. Flowers, wreaths, and immortelles—the spontaneous offerings of young and old—decked his coffin, as they do his grave. The universal tribute of respect, the solemn feeling that pervaded all alike, made an impression on the minds of some of the clergymen present that will not soon effaced; may it stimulate all of them to emulate their deceased brother in 'his labours of love, and works of faith in season and out of season,' and may they realise like him the texts on the borders of his pall 'Blessed are the dead which die in the Lord'; 'They rest from their labours, and their works follow.' "

The Parish Registers.

Very few parishes probably possess such a complete set of registers as Horsley. The earliest register bears marks of extreme age, and is quite 300 years old.

Many of its leaves are so stained by damp, that the writing is quite illegible, and in some places is quite washed away. If the Register had been left under a water spout it could not have presented a worse appearance, and no doubt was kept for many years in some place where the water streamed through the roof. Then the style of writing is difficult, and the spelling often inaccurate, that it is by no means easy to decipher its contents. Again the irregularity of its leaves clearly indicate that for years they must have been scattered abroad in some parish chest, and would have been lost altogether, had not some thoughtful person gathered them up and arranged them, and bound them in neat parchment covers. This register, as might be expected, after the description given above is exceedingly fragmentary, but it covers an important period of English History.

The earliest entry it contains is dated 1587, the latest 1674. It covers therefore a great part of the reign of Queen Elizabeth, the reigns of James I. and Charles I., the period of the Commonwealth, and more than half the reign of Charles II., and marks of the eventful times, during which it was in use, or not in use, are easily discernible. For example, the troublous times of Charles I., when civil war prevailed, are plainly shown by the sudden failure of entries for a number of years; the particulars of which will be given when that date is reached.

The following tabular statement of the number of Baptisms, Weddings, and Burials, in each year, so far as the entries are still extant, will give an idea of the population of the parish in those days. It will be convenient to divide the table, so as to make the sections coincide with the various reigns.

QUEEN ELIZABETH, DIED 1603.

DATE OF YEAR.	BAPTISMS.	WEDDINGS.	BURIALS.
1587	No record	No record	4 entries extant.
1588	—	—	13
1589	—	—	6
1590	6	—	9
1591	—	7	19
1592	22	5	5
1593	22	5	Register imperfect
1594	19	2	—
1595	13	3	—
1596	15	3	—
1597	14	6	—

DATE OF YEAR.	BAPTISMS.	WEDDINGS.	BURIALS.
1598	15	5	—
1599	15	6	—
1600	33	10	—
1601	21	5	—
1602	23	2	—

The years are dated from the 25th of March, with one exception, 1596, and not from January 1st as now. The year 1603 belongs entirely to James I. reign; who began to reign March 25th, 1603.

It is curious that in 1591 there were no baptisms. The year 1590 ends in the middle of a page, and the date immediately following is "Anno 1592." The other vacant spaces denote missing leaves of register.

The first entry is dated "7th day of November, 1587." It is the entry of a burial, but the name can hardly be deciphered. Three more entries succeed this, equally difficult to make out, and then follows "Anno 1588," "Thomas, the sonne of John Barnfielde, was buried the 2nd day of January;" and a little after appears plainly enough: "Richard Glastonbury was buried the 10th day of April;" again, "John Warkman was buried the 29th day of June, 1588;" again, "Henry Burde was buried the 5th day of Sept., 1588."

These four last names are remarkable as having representatives in the parish at this very day. And in the following pages many other names are found which are still known in the parish: Richard Gillman; Richard, sonne of Robert Drewe; William, son of John Parsloe; Agnes Guggins; Margaret Mody, (Moody) wife of Richard Moody: Elizabeth, daughter of Richard Birde; Thomas Samson, and Richard Samson; John Harrison; Elizabeth Sawyer; John Knight; Margary Gill. And on turning to the entries of baptisms and marriages, we find there were Lokiers, Newths, and Dyers, and Williames, and Clarks, and Warners, and Wakeleys, and Daniells, and Stephenses, and Clayfields, and Clofields, and Neales. Other names occur which are not now found in the parish, but are known in its vicinity, such as Gainer, Baydon, Paine, Cambridge, Jowling, Mill, Millwater, and Dowell.

As regards the names of the people, Horsley, in the days of Queen Elizabeth and the Spanish Armada differed but little from the Horsley of this 46th year of the reign of Queen Victoria. So little change in the course of 300 years is remarkable.

In this portion of the Horsley register, there is written across the margin of one of its leaves a paraphrase of the 131st Psalm, evidently being an attempt by some parish clerk of ancient days, as both the writing and spelling seem to show. The verse is difficult to read, but the following is as correct a copy as perhaps can be made.

"O Lord, i ham not puft in mind, i have no sovonful eye.
I doo not exdav sise my self in theings that be to high,
But as a child ywened is even from his mother's brest,
Soe have i Lord be haved my self in silence and in loss."

In the first line probably the word 'scornful' is meant. Tate and Brady in their metrical version of the Psalms use the word 'scornful,' but as we are supposing our parish clerk to have lived before the time of Tate and Brady, and certainly his rhyme is not like theirs, it is not unlikely that our clerk was following the version of Sternhold and Hopkins, which was published in 1562, and was probably in use at Horsley Church, until Tate and Brady superseded it.

By the same hand, in the margin of another page, are entered the baptisms of three of the Tranter family, viz., "Nathanioll, William, and Eliabeth."

And it is curious that on a page bearing the date 1603-4, there is an entry by a similar hand, written over other entries in very large style, "Robert Tranter was married."

Probably this humble-minded clerk was a Tranter, for Tranters held the office in succession for many years. Perhaps he was this very Robert Tranter, and when he wrote the paraphrase of the psalm, which has a sorrowful tone about it, he might have been mourning the death of a wife. The children baptized were probably his children, and the marriage recorded later on in such a bold hand was probably when he took to himself a second wife. If so, on this occasion he was considerably 'puft in mind,' or he would not have obliterated some four or five entries of baptisms to make room for the entry of his marriage.

JAMES I., FROM 1603 TO 1625.

	BAPTISMS.	WEDDINGS.	BURIALS.
1603	19	3	Register imperfect.
1604	20	4	,,
1605	25	4	,,
1606	20	8	,,
1607	26	10	,,
1608	22	4	,,
1609	25	5	15
1610	31	10	18

	BAPTISMS.	WEDDINGS.	BURIALS.
1611	23	6	6
1612	28	3	15
1613	23	4	19
1614	27	6	11
1615	31	7	15
1616	27	1	10
1617	22	1	18
1618	24	2	15
1619	30	9	8, partly deficient.
1620	20	1	Register imperfect.
1621	34	7	,,
1622	28	5	18
1623	19	5	14
1624	25	5	8

During this period we have a recurrence of familiar names as Bird, Wakeley, Moody, Dyer, Harrison, Clarke, Mill, Millwater, Gillman, Kembridge (Cambridge), Neal, Gugins, Lokier. And there appear others for the first time, all of which are still found in the parish as Turke, Peggler, Haines, Cooke, Hitchens, Pride, Nicholls, Plummer, Shipton, Dangerfield, Webb. There are also other names such as Ruff, Lymbrick, Penley, Chambers, Barnard, Bennett, Davys, Langdon, Barnwood, Lidyat, Osburne, Carter, Shepperd, Clutterbuck.

In the list of baptisms, it is interesting to observe the names of Webb, Turke, Bird, Wakeley, Dyer, following in consecutive order, probably the ancestors of those of same name still living side by side in Horsley.

In 1616 Shakespeare died. He seems during some portion of his life to have been connected with Dursley and its neighbourhood. And Mr. Blunt, the late Rector of Beverston, relates that in the register of that parish, there is an entry of a baptism in the year 1610:—

" Edward Shakespurre, the sunne of John Shakespurre and Margery his wife, was baptized the 17th day of September. Godfathers: Edward Eastcourt, Francis Savage. Godmother: Mary Eastcourt."

There is, however, no record in the Horsley register of any Shakespear at this early period—though curiously enough there have been two distinct families of the name resident in the parish, viz., the family of the late Sir Richmond Shakespear, at Horsley

Court, which left in 1881, and a family of the same name still residing at Walkley Wood.

CHARLES I.

The reign of Charles I. dates from 1625 to 1649, but from 1642 to the end of the reign civil war prevailed, and in consequence the country was thrown into confusion. It is interesting to notice that this period of confusion is clearly marked in the parish register— for after the year 1640 there is a sudden failure of entries, and which continues for about twelve years. There are indeed a few entries, but these do not occur in chronological order, and seem to have been made by some unauthorized person.

Judging from the state of the register after 1640, one is led to think the parish was without a clergyman from that date to the end of the civil wars. And yet as the civil war did not begin until 1642, and the failure of entries begins in 1640, the absence of a clergyman during these two years must be accounted for by some other cause. A reference to the List of Vicars, already given, will show that in 1640 Richard Horton was presented to the vicarage of Horsley by King Charles I., but it is highly probable that he never came to the parish.

The following is a list of the entries of the Baptisms, Weddings, and Burials which took place down to the year 1640, and then follows the period of confusion :—

	BAPTISMS.	WEDDINGS.	BURIALS.
1625.	20	1	Register exists but the
1626.	23	3	entries are illegible and
1627.	25	3	the parchment is soft
1628.	25	9	like wash leather.
1629.	35	1	
1630.	27	3	
1631.	23	2	From 1627 to the end
1632.	9	3	of 1637 the register is
1633.	46	4	missing.
1634.	25	3	
1635.	29	6	
1636.	33	3	
1637.	19	5	2
1638.	21	7	18
1639.	14	7	22
1640.	35	12	25

The number of Baptisms under date 1633 doubtless contains

PAGE OF ANCIENT REGISTER.

some belonging to the former year, and the register seems to show
some were entered by an after-thought.

There are four entries of Baptisms of interest, and to which
attention is called by an index in the margin, ☞ *sic*, viz. :—

1635.—Samuel, son of Samuel Hieron, Minister, baptized April 19.
1636.—Nathaniel, son of Samuel Hieron, baptized 26th May.
1637.—Anne, daughter of Samuel Hieron, baptized 25th December.
1640.—Queenborowe, the daughter of Samuel Hieron, Minister,
     baptized 6th August.

There are several names which appear in the register for the first
time in this reign, and which are still found in the parish, as Antill,
Teakle, Tanner, Arundell, Harvey, Evans, and Hurne.

Other names appear also for the first time, although not now
represented, as Frankom, Wilkins, Horwood, Tibbs, Hiller,
Howelder, Stringer, Knight, Wintle, Curtis, Benson.

The name Harley also occurs, which still survives undoubtedly in
the name Harley Wood.

PERIOD OF CONFUSION.

Nothing but the art of photography can convey to the mind of
those who have not an opportunity of examining the Horsley
registers for themselves, the utter confusion of entries which
prevails for a space of twelve or thirteen years, viz., from the
beginning of 1641 to the end of the year 1653. And this period
singularly coincides with a time of confusion and trouble to Church
and State.

In 1642, civil war broke out between King and Parliament, and
continued until 1649, in the January of which year King Charles
was executed. Then followed the Abolition of the Monarchy and
of the House of Lords, and the government of the country was
committed to a 'Council of State. In the year 1653, on the 16th of
December, Oliver Cromwell was proclaimed Lord-Protector of the
Commonwealth of England, and from the March following, in 1654,
the register is again well kept and the entries follow on in regular
order.

To give an account of the particulars of the register during the
same period we will take first the baptisms.

BAPTISMS.

The entries for the year 1640 conclude with an entry made on 21st
of March in that year, and then a line is drawn across the page, and
so preparation is made for the entries of another year as follows :

"Anno Domi 1641."

Immediately under this date two baptisms are entered, one on March 22nd, the other on October 10th, but the names are difficult to decipher, except that the last looks like "Nathaniell Tekell"; after this:

"John, the son of John Jones, was baptized the 13 day of ffebuary, 164—." (last figure obliterated.)

"William, son of John dier, was baptized the 8th day of March, 164—."

"Mary, daughter of Nathanoll Huthins (probably Hitchens), baptized, April, 1648."

"Joseph Mayo, sonne of Henry Mayo, was baptized the 19th day of November, 1648."

"1644."

"Sarah, daughter of ffrancis Langley, was baptized 29th day of September."

Then follows another baptism in "1645," and another dated "1654." At the top of the next page is written

"Baptizings, Anno Domi, 1652."

And sixteen entries follow belonging to that year. And two others are inserted in the middle of the page, dated "1653." Another also so inserted is a record of birth only.

"Mary, daughter of Nathanioll Long? was *borne* the 15th day of October, 1553." This singular entry may indicate the first appear- of Baptists in the parish. Some of the names in this page are tolerably legible, as "John, the sonne of John dyer, baptised 17 day of September, 1648."

The names "Lockier," "Barker," "Clarke," "Wilkins" are also visible. And "Abigall, the daughter of Richard Antill, was baptised the 13th day of March, 1653."

And at the foot of the page is an entry in a very bold hand;

"Isaac Kidron, son of Samuel Hieron, baptised Nov. 8, 1654."

WEDDINGS.

During this time of social discord and civil war there is not a single wedding entered in the register.

The entries for the year 1640 continue to the foot of one page, and on the next page of the same leaf are given the weddings of the year 1654.

BURIALS.

Here again the entries are regular to the end of 1640, *i.e.*, the

25th of March—and extend a little over two-thirds of the page; then a line is drawn, and under the date of next year as

"*Burials, Anno Domi*, 1641."
But no burials are entered. On top of next page is written
"*Buryals*, 1652."
And two entries occur in month of July. Again a line is drawn, and underneath is written

"*Burialles that hath bene set downe since the Act of parlyment concerning Registering from the 16th of March, 1653, By me, John Dier, sowrne (sworn) Register of Horsley.*
But notwithstanding this statement no entries occur for the year 1653. The next following is dated May, 1654, after which time entries are made regularly.

HORSLEY DURING THE CIVIL WAR.

There can be no doubt that during the Civil War of Charles I. reign, the country in the immediate neighbourhood of Horsley was in a very unsettled state, and the inhabitants of the parish must often have witnessed the passing to and fro of both Royalist and Parliamentarian troops. It is also just possible that they were subjected to annoyance and suffering from the frequent incursion of these rival armies. The condition of the register shows plainly the occasional offices of the Church were suspended during this period, and probably many of the parishioners sought a temporary and safer home elsewhere.

The Rev. J. H. Blunt, the Rector of Beverston, tells us in his History of "Dursley and its Neighbourhood," that "when Gloucestershire came to take so large a share in the miserable rebellion against Charles I., the king took possession of Beverston Castle as a commanding post on the edge of the disaffected manufacturing district, which lay in the cloth weaving valleys, between it and Gloucester. Malmesbury, Tetbury, and Wotton-under-Edge, were also fortified posts." Horsley, therefore, being in such close proximity to three of these Royalist camps, and lying between them and a disaffected district, if not forming a part of it,—for the Lord of the Manor was a Parliamentarian,—we may well suppose it to have been greatly disturbed by the contending parties. And Horsley men went forth to the war: for Mr. Blunt says the parish register of Beverston contains an entry, "John Eires, of Horsley, a Souldier of the Castle, was buryed the 23rd of Novemb., 1643." If the Lord of the Manor was a Parliamentarian, there were Royalists among the people of the place.

"As the war went on," says Mr. Blunt, "the northern part of Gloucestershire fell more and more into the hands of the rebels, and as Beverston commanding the rich clothiers of Stroudwater, hindered the southward carriage of the manufacturers, by which these disloyal clothiers became rich, it was a great object to get it out of the hand of the king." Now which way did these rich clothiers send their goods to the southward, so as to come under the observation of the Royalists at Beverston? One naturally thinks of the road by Tetbury Lane and Chavenage. An old map gives a continuation of Tetbury Lane by back of Barton End in direction of Cranmore, until it comes out into the high road just above Beverston village. The Vestry map continues this road part of the way.

By this road Parliamentarian troops passed on their way to and from Beverston. Mr. Blunt continues, "Early in 1644, Colonel Massey, the Parliamentarian Commander at Gloucester, marched thence to Beverston, with a party of 300 foot and 80 horsemen. The horse soldiers were sent on to Tetbury, where Horatio Cary, the governor, with his whole regiment, were put to flight by them, with a loss of fourteen men slain or taken prisoners." Probably these came from Gloucester, by way of Rodborough, Inchborough, Nailsworth, and then by Tetbury Lane across to Cranmore and Beverston.

Whilst the cavalry went on to Tetbury, Colonel Massey attacked Beverston. Corbet, an old Puritan writer says, "He brought up his men and two sakers against Beverston Castle, where, having surrounded it, he planted his guns within pistol shot of the gate, and gave fire several times. Fifty musketeers ran up to the gate at noonday and fired a petard, which nevertheless failed in execution. Those from within threw grenades amongst our men, but hurt none, who, although thereby forced from the gate, yet they ran up the second time, being open to the full shot of a secure enemy, and brought off the petard with much gallantry. The design was not feasible for a quick despatch, for the gate was barricaded within. The night came on, and those remote parts did promise no security to so small a party, likewise the state of the city required them nearer home; wherefore, after twelve hours the party was drawn off, retreating towards Wotton-under-Edge."

"The Governor of Beverston, at this time, was Colonel Oglethorpe, and very shortly after, he, with six of his troopers, was captured by seven of Massey's soldiers. Colonel Massey was then in Herefordshire, busily occupied in reducing that county for his party, but when the news reached him of the capture of the governor of Beverston, seeing his chance to get possession of the Castle, and so to relieve the rich clothiers of Stroudwater from the bondage and terror of the Royalists, he determined to make an effort to take it. He had paid a temporary visit to Gloucester, but at two o'clock at night he set off for Ross, and commanded his foot over the Severn at Newnham Passage, whilst his horse marched by Gloucester, and after a forced march, occupying the night and day, he rendezvoused within three miles of Beverston, on Thursday, 23rd May, 1644."— *Blunt*.

One would like to know the spot, but it must certainly have been somewhere within the boundary of Horsley Parish. There are two ways by which his troops might have come from Newnham, either by the old road before spoken of over Frocester Hill, and then by Nympsfield, Horsley, and Hay Lane, or by the Woodchester Valley to Nailsworth, and Tetbury Lane. The Cavalry coming from Gloucester would doubtless take the latter route. The rendezvous, 3 miles from Beverston, was probably some point between Barton End and Beverston. The Picked Stone must have been a prominent landmark in those days when the country was open, and as regards its distance from Beverston, its neighbourhood would agree well with the record.

From this halting place Colonel Massey marched quickly to Beverston. The garrison were taken by surprise, and surrendered before midnight. Colonel Massey then went on to Malmesbury, which place was taken by him two or three days later.

As a reward for these exploits, on May 31st, 1644, the House of Commons ordered that the Town of Malmesbury and the Castle of Beverston, as to the government of them, shall be left wholly to the disposal of Col. Massey. Col. Henry Stevens, whom Mr. Blunt supposes to have been a relative of Nathaniel Stevens, of Chavenage House, was then made by Col. Massey governor of Beverston. But this Col. Stevens seems to have been guilty of great indiscretion, for he left Beverston without orders to go to the relief of Rowden House, between Devizes and Malmesbury, and was there shut up by a bold dash of the Royalists. Beverston, therefore, was in danger of recapture by the Royalists, but was relieved by a party of horse sent up from Gloucester.

From this time Beverston seems to have been retained by the Parliamentarians; and the neighbouring House of Chavenage seems also to have been in their hands, and was visited by three great leaders of their party. Three upper rooms in Chavenage House

have the names of Cromwell, Lord Essex, and Ireton, affixed to
their doors, as memorials that they were once occupied by these
great generals of the Parliamentarian army. "Cromwell's Hat" was
one of the curiosities offered by the Auctioneers at a Sale of the
contents of Chavenage in 1870. As tradition speaks thus of a visit
to the parish by Cromwell, so it seems Charles I. passed very near it.
Mr. Blunt says, "On Sunday, July 14th, 1644, King Charles passed
by Beverston at the head of 7000 troops, horse and foot, on the
road from Gloucester to Bath. The King slept at Sapperton on the
night of the 13th, and reached Badminton the next day."

NATHANIEL STEPHENS, OF CHAVENAGE.

This gentleman was Squire of Chavenage, and Lord of the Manor
of Horsley, in those troublous times of King Charles I. He was
Knight of the Shire for the County of Gloucester, therefore had a
seat in Parliament. He is described as a man not so much opposed
to the office of King, as to the royal exactions, a friend to the
Church, but dreading in the revived ceremonies of Archbishop Laud,
a return to the Papal dominion in England. When the Civil War
broke out he was induced to appear in arms at the head of a
regiment of horse in behalf of the Parliament.

From a speech made by him in Parliament, and given in full in
the preface to Huntley's poem on Chavenage, it-is clear that at first
he did not approve of the execution of the king. His words were:—
"Some speak of a strange cure; they would cut off the head to
save the body, but as that is impossible in the natural body, so it
is unlikely in the politic body." His family was connected by
marriage with Ireton and Cromwell: but we are told their more
secret councils were not made known to him until the time
approached for their execution.

Stephens was keeping Christmas at Chavenage, when, in the midst
of the festivity, Ireton arrived with a view to press his instant
attendance in Parliament to support by his vote and influence the
intended measures against the life of Charles. His sister is reported
to have urged him strongly to withhold his voice, and in a moment
of enthusiasm to have prophesied the extinction of his line in case
he became implicated in the murder of the king.

Ireton, assisted by Robert Stephens, brother to the Colonel, spent
the night in entreating him to comply; and at length, though
Nathaniel's feelings were in agreement with his sister's arguments,
and though he even imagined himself to have been warned in a
vision not to be assisting in the death of the king, he nevertheless
suffered himself to be overruled, and giving a reluctant acqui-

CHAVENAGE

escence, departed with Ireton. In the May following, he was
seized with a fatal sickness. On his deathbed he is stated to have
called togther his relations, in order to take his last adieus, and to
express his regret for his participation in the execution of the king.
Then follows the legend as given by Huntley:—"When all his rela-
tives had assembled, and their several well-known equipages were
crowding the courtyard, and the sick man was now breathing his
last, the household were surprised to observe that another coach
ornamented in even more than the gorgeous embellishments of that
splendid period, and drawn by black horses, was approaching
the door in great solemnity. When it arrived, making a short stay,
the door of the vehicle opened in some unseen manner, and clad in
his shroud, the shade of the Colonel glided into the carriage, and
the door instantly closing upon him, the coach rapidly, but silently
withdrew from the house, not however with such speed, but there
was time to perceive the driver was a beheaded man, that he was
arrayed in the royal vestments, with the garter moreover on his
leg, and the star of that illustrious order upon his breast. No
sooner had the coach arrived at the gateway of the Manor Court
than the whole appearance vanished in flames of fire. The story
further maintains that to this day every lord of Chavenage dying in
the manor-house takes his departure in this ominous conveyance."

The last surviving male descendant was Sir Philip Stephens,
Baronet, M.P., a Lord of the Admiralty, who died 1809.

THE PARISH REGISTERS (CONTINUED).

Oliver Cromwell was Lord Protector from December 16th, 1653,
to September 3rd, 1658. Richard Cromwell succeeded until April
22nd, 1659. Commonwealth restored 1659. The Monarchy 1660.

A.D.	BAPTISMS.	WEDDINGS.	BURIALS.
1654.	34	14	27
1655.	44	11	17
1656.	31	1	13
1657.	36	1	17
1658.	9	2	none.
1659.	5	1	1

It will be seen from the above table that in the early years of
Cromwell the Register was tolerably well kept, but after the close
of 1658 confusion again appears.

The entries of Baptisms for 1658-59-60 are made by various
hands, and mixed together in the most deplorable fashion, although
they are all written on the same page.

At the top of this page there is the name "Thomas, the sonne of Gilles Bishop, was baptised the 14th day of Sept." This entry is repeated lower down the page in large hand, and the date of year is added, (1659).

"John, the son of Nathaniell Tranter, was baptized the 14th day of September, 1659."

Other names appear, which may be of interest to the present generation, as

"William, son of William Hide, baptised 30th day of December, 1655."

"John, the son of William Humphreys, was baptized the 6th day of January."

"Mary, daughter of Charles Nuth, was baptized 16th day of October, 1657."

Old names also re-appear, as Webb, Wilkins, Clarke, Hiller, Harrison, Millwater, Neale, etc. Some names seem fresh to the parish, as Halling, Holliday, Dowell, English.

The marriage entries are also interesting, as showing a new system of registering them, and also the prevalence of Puritan terms; thus

"Richard Holliday and Reboakath Franklin whare published three severall *Lord's Days* in Horsley's Church, and maryed the 13th day of Aprill, 1654."

Witneffe, John Hiller."

"John Mills and Edeth Sheppeard whare published three severall *Lord's Days* in Horsley's Church, and maryed the 24th day of September, 1654, by Thos. Bearde."

"Nathaniel Chambers, and Shuana Pride, whare published three severall *Lord's Days* in Horsley's Church, one the twenty-one day, and one the twenty-eighteh day of October, and one the foureth day of No'ember, 1655, and maryed the foreteenth day of No'ember, 1655, before me, one of the Justices of the Peace for the sayd County."

No signature.

"Philip Webb, and Hester Chambers, whare published three severall *Lord's Days* in Horsley's Church, and maryed the 25th day of December, 1655, in witnesse whereof.

John Webb, OO his mark.

John Danoll.   Nath. Cripps."

We may notice, with reference to these entries, that the Certifying Magistrate did not always sign his name, but the signature of Nath. Cripps is of frequent occurrence. Also, it is interesting to observe that every man and woman who could not write, had *his* or *her mark*, and by no means kept to the orthodox cross, as now-a-days.

It will be difficult for a printer to represent these marks, but some of them resemble the letters of the alphabet. One signs his mark H, another as above OO, another O, another M, another I, another M.

These following entries are also interesting, as evidently referring to ancestors of present parishioners :

"Thomas Bishop and Margaret Horwood were published three severall *Lord's Days* in Horsley's Church, one the fifteen day of November, one the 2nd day and one the 9th day of December, and maryed the 27th day of December by me, one of the Justices of the Peace of the County, this 27th day of December, 1655.

(Witness scarcely legible.)   Nath. Cripps."

In the above entry there is an error, for evidently the " fifteenth day " of November, ought to be the 25th.

"Charles Nuth and Mary Barnefield, were published three severall *Lord's days*, in Horsley Church, one the third day, one the tenth day, and one the seventeenth day of February, 1655, and were maryed the seventh day of Aprill, 1656, by one of the Justices of the Peace for the said County, on day and yeare abovesaid, in witness whereof."

The following are also interesting, and are in a very distinct hand :—

"Nathanael Hall, Minister, and Alice, *alias* Rebeckah, the daughter of Samuel Cambridge, were published three several Sundays in the Parish Church of Horsley, by John Dyer, then Register, and were maryed the 14th day of July, 1659."

THE REIGN OF CHARLES II., FROM 1660 TO 1685.

The Parish Register for this period exhibits almost as great confusion and neglect as it does during the period of the Civil Wars of Charles I.

The entries are as nearly as possible as follows :—

A.D.	BAPTISMS.	WEDDINGS.	BURIALS.
1660.	2	4	none.
1661.	8	2	16
1662.	15	none.	18
1663.	7	,,	21
1664.	1	,,	21
1665.	26	11	14
1666.	1	11	illegible.
1667.	1	11	none.

A.D.	BAPTISMS.	WEDDINGS.	BURIALS.
1668.	1	11	1
1669.	none.	none.	none.
1670.	1	,,	,,
1671.	none.	,,	1
1672.	1	,,	none.
1673.	1	,,	,,
1674.	none.	1	,,
1675.	,,	,,	,,
1676.	,,	,,	,,
1677.	,,	,,	,,
1678.	,,	,,	,,
1679.	,,	,,	,,
1680.	1	,,	,,
1681.	none.	,,	,,
1682.	1	,,	,,
1683.	none.	,,	,,
1684.	2	,,	,,
1685.	1	,,	,,

It is evident that the Vicar of the parish during part of this time, was Mr. Nathanaël Hall, for there appear the following entries:—

"1660. Nathanaël, the son of Mr. Nathanaël Hall, Minister of this parish, was baptized the 5th day of Aug."

"1660. Nathanaël, ye son of Mr. Nathanaël Hall, Minister of Horsley, was buryed ye 16th day of March, 1660." (Old Style.)

"1661. Elizabeth, daughter of Nathanaël Hall, was baptised 20th day of October."

"1663. Mrs. Rebekah, the wife of Mr. Nathanaël Hall, was buryed 30th July."

"Nathaniel Hall, Minister of Horsley, being published—— dayes, was maryed to Mrs. Anna, the daughter of——, of the same parish, on the 18th day of February, 1665."

"Mr. Hall, of Beverstone."

There are a few other entries in the register for this period, which require some notice.

There are five entries of baptisms of the Tranters, grouped together on one page, and dated respectively, 1672, 1650, 1667, 1671, and 1674. On another page there is a marriage entry of the Tranters, dated 1666, and a burial entry dated 1671. These are all entered irregularly, and evidently from memory. The scribblings of the Tranter family have been noticed before, as occurring in time of Elizabeth and James I., but thesè last are in a very different style of writing, and evidently belonging to a late generation. Perhaps the office of parish clerk was filled by members of the Tranter family for nearly a century : hence the repeated scribblings of this name, from the days of Elizabeth, down to the reign of Charles II.

On another page are two entries belonging to a family named Terrett.

"Henry Terrett was baptised the second day of February, in the year of our Lord God 1674."

"Michael ? Terrett was baptised the 4th day of February, in the year of our Lord God 1669.

Before proceeding further, it should be mentioned that the oldest register which has hitherto been the subject of notice, and which dates from the year 1587, concludes with the year 1668; but there are a few isolated entries of later date, down to the year 1674, and even one or two baptisms of the Teakle's, belonging to the year 1714.

The next register is dated on the cover, from the year 1680 to 1717, but the early part contains a few entries, here and there dated as far back as 1672. The early part of this register was very irregularly kept, and it is not until we reach the year 1695 that we find anything like order. We may well conclude therefore, that no part of the original register is missing, but that the irregularity was caused by the troubled times, through which Church and State were still passing.

Bigland, in his list of Vicars, gives the name of Collins, who was appointed Vicar in 1690, by King William III., and it is at this date another word appears in the register, in lieu of the word baptisms. Thus we have at the top of the page "The *Christianings* in the year of the Lord 1690," but it is not until the year 1695 that any great improvement is made in keeping the register, and then the pages are respectively and regularly headed, "Christianings," "Weddings," "Burialls."

The summary of entries continued—

JAMES II., 1685—1688.

A.D.	BAPTISMS.	WEDDINGS.	BURIALS.
1685.	1	none.	none.
1686.	1	1	,,
1687.	8	none.	,,
1688.	9	,,	,,

46

WILLIAM III., 1688—1702.

A.D.	CHRISTIANINGS.	WEDDINGS.	BURIALS.
1689.	8	none.	none.
1690.	7	,,	,,
1691.	8	,,	,,
1692.	4	,,	,,
1693.	2	,,	,,
1694.	1	1	,,
1695.	40	8	21
1696.	20	2	19
1697.	25	5	19
1698.	21	6	21
1699.	9	10	11
1700.	none.	6	none.
1701.	3	11	,,
1702.	none.	7	,,

The following names, among others, appear in the register during this period :—

Webb, Howel, Tainton, Kinton, Sansom, Horwood, Blackmore, Craft, King, Fryer, Brinkworth, Whiteway, Plummer, Guy, Parke, Crumb.

And for the benefit of the Hides,[1] whose pedigree has been in such request of late we may quote the following entries—"Sarah, daughter of William Hyde, and Elizabeth his wife, was baptized Feb. 28th, 1696."

"William Hide was buried Oct. 28th, 1696."

"Widow Hide was buried May 19th, 1697."

---

1 Many years ago, about the middle of the last century, certain brothers of the name of Hyde left this neighbourhood—as it is supposed—and went to India, where they amassed a large fortune; but they died without a will, and their money was left in the Bank of England. No claimant appears to have come forward for many years, and the property has gone on accumulating up to the present time, and has now reached an enormous sum (says an American newspaper.) The fortune, awaiting claimants, has attracted considerable attention both in America and our own country; and many enquiries are being made in various places respecting the pedigree of the Hydes. Horsley has received its share of attention, and the registers have been searched repeatedly, in answer to enquiries, both from America and elsewhere, for records of the Hyde family.

Certainly, from the early part of the last century down to its close, the name Hyde is of frequent recurrence, but after that date it is but rarely found; probably many of the name left the parish and settled in America or elsewhere. As they were mostly weavers, and the cloth trade at the close of the last century was very bad, they may have been obliged to go elsewhere in search of employment.

"The child of John Hide was buried Dec. 9th, 1697."

"Margery, daughter of Thomas Hide was baptized March 29th, 1710."

"Richard, son of Nathaniell Stephens, Esq., was baptized July 21st, Anno Domini, 1698."

Mention of the Hamlet of Newmarket occurs for the first time in the following entry :—

"Joseph, the son of Thomas and Martha Arnold, baptized 21st April, 1697, of Newmarket."

Bigland says "The persons summoned by the heralds in 1682-1683, were Thomas Davis and John Hillier, Gent." The name Hillier constantly recurs in the register about this time.

QUEEN ANNE, 1702—1714.

The following is a summary of entries in the parish registers, in this reign :

A.D.	CHRISTIANINGS.	WEDDINGS.	BURIALS.
1702.	none.	7	no entries.
1703.	7	10	,,
1704.	25	9	14
1705.	25	13	26
1706.	26	no entries.	35
1707.	12	16	22
1708.	7	16	16
1709.	1	10	26
1710.	4	5	34
1711.	9	5	47
1712.	12	4	38
1713.	12	16	11
1714.	4	9	19

It is evident from the foregoing list and the condition of the register, that the register was still very carelessly kept. The burial entries are, however, more carefully made than the others, owing, no doubt, to the fact that certificates had now to be given that the dead were "buried in woollen."

The following entries, which occur in the margin of the register, may be of interest.

"No affidavit being made for Dinah Ayres, or James Bird, notice was given of the neglect to Mr. Birt, overseer, March 11, 1710."

Again. "Notice was given to Mr. Claivel, Churchwarden, that no affidavit was made for Thos. Hyde and Elizabeth Baiden, May 3rd, 1711."

Again. "Certified Aug. 23rd, that no affidavit was brought for Elizabeth Knight."

Again. "Certified to the Churchwarden that no affidavit was brought of William Lokier's being buried in woollen, Aug. 23."

It will be observed in the list of burials that the number of interments for the years 1710, 1711, 1712, was unusually high; it suggests the idea that perhaps some terrible epidemic prevailed in the village at that time.

The following entries of baptisms are also of interest:—

"Maria, daughter of Mr. John Gyles, Minister, was born 16th day of Jany., 1704."

"Frances, the daughter of Nathanael Stephens, Esq., Novr. 13th, 1703."

Other names appear, some for the first time, some after an interval, as Bown, Rickets, Selwyn. Horwood, Browning, Creed, Cromwell, Steel, Peglar, Drew, Hopkins, Mabbett, Daw, Kimish, Leonard, Gillman, Garlick.

GEORGE I., 1714—1727.

The following is the summary:—

A.D.	CHRISTENINGS.	WEDDINGS.	BURIALS.
1715.	entries missing.	6	19
1716.	10	13	19
1717.	34	15	11
1718.	28	21	11
1719.	29	14	18
1720.	28	5	25
1721.	30	17	31
1722.	25	15	30
1723.	38	17	33
1724.	35	12	23
1725.	36	11	17
1726.	26	11	27
1727.	22	15	33

There is very little change in the names of the parishioners at this period. The following seem to appear in the Register for the first time:—Edge, Astman, Farmer, Marmon, Fortune, Heaven, Clift, Curthois, Skirton, Cole, Bartholomew, Window.

George II., 1727-60.

A.D.	CHRISTIANINGS.	WEDDINGS.	BURIALS.
1728.	15	9	33
1729.	18	12	36
1730.	29	12	17
1731.	35	19	17
1732.	44	24	28
1733.	54	10	19
1734.	52	17	22
1735.	58	11	39
1736.	42	20	40
1737.	45	12	38
1738.	46	22	48
1739.	47	25	46
1740.	42	13	47
1741.	22	12	64
1742.	29	16	40
1743.	56	23	47
1744.	52	22	23
1745.	44	20	30
1746.	44	22	28
1747.	47	14	26
1748.	59	19	38
1749.	41	47	28
1750.	54	20	27
1751.	32	15	24
1752.	45	17	39
1753.	45	14	38
1754.	60	22	35
1755.	46	23	20
1756.	38	9	36
1757.	36	5	37
1758.	48	23	38
1759.	53	22	60
1760.	70	21	32

It is evident from the above summaries that during the reign of George II. the population of Horsley increased considerably.

The following names occur in this period, and may be of interest: Blackwell, Cottle, Farmiloe, (spelt Farmula) Brunket, Griffin,

E

Mallard, Witchell, Remmington, Hanks, Fletcher, Loyd, Leonard, Parnel, Risby, Vevers, Churchess, [1] Nelms, Axon.

The following entries are also interesting:—

"Baptism.—April 26, 1737. Edward Webb, son of Paul and Elizabeth Castelman."

And the burial of this same Edward Webb Castelman is recorded Sept. 8, 1760.

"Baptism.—Nov. 21, 1738. Elizabeth, daughter of Paul and Elizabeth Castleman."

"Burial.—1728. Mary, wife of Cornelius Gingell, Oct. 9th, on which day Callcourt Barn was burnt with lightning." Kingscote Windmill was similarly destroyed not many years ago.

"Burial.—Ap. 9, 1729. Charles Smith, Gent."

1732.—"Wedding.—John Pegler and Ann Thomas were half married Aug. 11th. I proceeded no further because they paid me but one-half, 2s. 6d."

I imagine that the wedding ceremony was proceeded with as far as the giving of the ring, when, according to the ancient custom, the Clergyman and Clerk's fees were laid with the ring on the book, but John Pegler giving no more than 2s. 6d., and declining to give the proper fees the ceremony abruptly terminated, and the bride and bridegroom went their way only half-married.

"Burial.—March 10, 1738. Paul, son of Richard Wallington, Vicar.

,, 13, 1738. Alicia, wife of Richard Wallington, Vicar.

,, 18, 1738. John, son of Richard Wallington, Vicar."

A tablet, still on the Church wall just inside the north door on the right hand, also records the above sad events.

In May, 1754, a new law came into operation which required the marriages to be registered in a separate book. This new register was a combination of the modern banns book and marriage register, except that the information then required was not so full as now. On the first page is the title: A Marriage Register Book according to Act of Parliament: London: Printed for Thomas Lownds, near Exeter Exchange. MDCCLIV.

Two important events of a domestic character belong to this reign. Until the year 1751, the Julian Calendar, or Old Style was

1 The cottages known as The Nelms doubtless derive their name from this family, who in the last century might possibly have lived there, and not as some suppose from a corruption of the word Elms,

followed, which made the years begin at the 25th of March, and also made the English reckoning of time eleven days behind that of the continent, as corrected by the great movements of nature. Hence it was enacted by Parliament that Jan. 1 after this year should be considered the beginning of the New Year, and called 1752, and the day following the 2nd of September should be called the 14th of September. Both these changes are observed in the Horsley Register, for after the year 1751, the years are dated from Jan. 1, instead of from March 25th as previously.

An entry of burial occurs on the very day the change was made, Jan. 1st, 1752. "William Selwyn, aged 94." And there was a wedding on the day following the 2nd of Sept., which according to the old style would have been called the 3rd, but by the new style was reckoned the 14th. "Sept. 14th, 1752. Nathanael Window and Mary Lockyer." There are no entries of any sort for any date between the 2nd September and the 14th, 1752. We cannot tell how the change was received at Horsley, but we know that in many places the common people thought they were robbed of eleven days by the Parliament, and, "give us back the eleven days we have been robbed of" became the popular election cry in the county of Oxford. The latter part of this reign was also marked by the revival preaching of Whitfield and Wesley, but there is no sign of their work afforded by our registers. The Methodists were very fond of giving extraordinary bible names to their children, and the lists of baptisms in some parish registers show plainly by the sudden increase of such names that Wesley's influence was felt, but, with the exception of the names Zaccheus and Jonah, there is nothing unusual to lead us to suppose the influence of the Methodists was much felt in Horsley.

GEORGE III., 1760—1820.

A.D.	CHRISTIANINGS.	WEDDINGS.	BURIALS.
1761.	39	17	34
1762.	47	8	41
1763.	45	23	29
1764.	46	11	42
1765.	45	20	59
1766.	44	11	58
1767.	32	20	31
1768.	31	16	47
1769.	30	13	40
1770.	48	18	39
1771,	34	18	28

A.D.	CHRISTIANINGS.	WEDDINGS.	BURIALS.
1772.	46	15	39
1773.	20	13	38
1774.	31	21	40
1775.	29	13	63
1776.	41	32	29
1777.	37	15	36
1778.	46	22	46
1779.	27	16	36
1780.	39	16	30
1781.	45	16	48
1782.	33	16	33
1783.	25	15	36
1784.	27	15	52
1785.	23	17	46
1786.	31	24	56
1787.	32	25	25
1788.	42	31	24
1789.	45	21	25
1790.	52	14	30
1791.	48	32	38
1792.	43	29	31
1793.	44	14	31
1794.	49	18	31
1795.	64	19	41
1796.	49	24	21
1797.	51	19	36
1798.	48	25	44
1799.	41	24	33
1800.	40	17	22

In the year 1774, the name of the officiating Clergyman is for the first time appended, and in this case is "Richard Davies, Vicar."

In 1794, is the christening of Robert Henry, son of Rev. Robert Nicholl.

In the year 1798, the term "Christianings" gives place for the word "Baptisms." The Rev. J. Dudley Fosbrook was then Curate. In 1790, there was the christening of "Mary, daughter of William and Mary Hiron, from Avening parish," who might have been a descendant of the old family of Hierons.

In the list of burials for 1783, opposite a burial entry of October 15th, is a note: "N.B.—Here the duty on burials first took place,"

This tax on burials was exceedingly cruel, and how the poor suffered by it is manifest by the notes in the margin of the register for the next few years, indicating the funerals conducted at the expense of the parish. It 1784, out of 52 burials, 29, or more than half were "by the parish." In 1785, out of 46 burials, 18 were by the parish. 1786, out of 56 burials, 31 were by the parish. In 1787, there were 25 burials, and 7 of them were by the parish. In 1788, there were 24 burials, and 10 by the parish; and so for several successive years the parish funerals are indicated, but the proportion gets less, being in these later years about one-third of the whole. When this burial tax was abolished there is nothing in the register to show. These entries also indicate the excessive poverty in the parish at that period. Now the parish funerals would not exceed about one-twelfth of the whole, but, no doubt, the existence of our present Benefit Societies and Clubs has done much to reduce the number of paupers' funerals. There are a few burial entries of interest in this period, especially of the Castleman family, to whom Horsley is indebted for some of its endowments.

In 1765, April 3. "Paul Castleman, Esq., Gent."

In 1771, Feb. 8. "Jonathan, son of Paul Castleman, Esq."

In 1786, Oct. 10. "Paul Castleman, Esq."

In 1792, Jan. 27. "Elizabeth, wife of John Remmington, Esq."

In 1793, Jan. 23. "Mr. William Harvey, Gent., Attorney at law."

In 1794, Oct. 5. "The Honble. Margaret Castleman, relict of Paul Castleman, Esq."

In 1798 July 9. "Ann Giles, who died from excessive drunkenness."

The Marriage Register, which was ordered by Act of Parliament in 1754, by its giving fuller information than had previously been the custom, enables us to get an idea of the domestic life of the people. In the latter half of the last century, the great majority of the Horsley people were either 'weavers,' 'broadweavers,' 'cloth-workers,' or 'scribblers;' occasionally we meet with a 'shearman,' and a 'saddle-tree' maker. And in 1757 there is the record of the marriage of one John Ball, a 'peruke-maker,' reminding us of the fashion of those days.

In the year 1780 there is a marriage entry of one Samuel Beddington, sergeant in the " Elgin Fencibles."

Robert Tranter seems to have been the Parish Clerk from about the year 1758 to 1767. John Sansom succeeded the above from 1767 to 1779. Robert Sansom followed the above from 1779 to 1821, in which year he was succeeded by his son, Richard Sansom, and father of our present Sexton. The office of Clerk or Sexton has been held by members of the Sansom family for more than 100 years. A member of the Tranter family also still survives in the parish.

A.D.	BAPTISMS.	WEDDINGS.	BURIALS.
1801.	40	24	33
1802.	52	39	31
1803.	45	34	23
1804.	56	22	19
1805.	60	32	30
1806.	57	15	32
1807.	29	26	38
1808.	35	19	32
1809.	45	29	25
1810.	29	17	28
1811.	62	20	37
1812.	54	15	29
1813.	39	16	17
1814.	41	19	42
1815.	46	36	31
1816.	72	27	33
1817.	53	34	28
1818.	64	36	51
1819.	57	40	33
1820.	63	42	20

With the exception of several notes, made by the hand of the Rev. F. D. Fosbrook, which will be given separately farther on, there is nothing in the register during the above period worthy of special mention.

A glance at the number of baptisms and weddings towards the close of George III. reign, will show that the population of Horsley was then rapidly increasing. The weddings had more than doubled since the beginning of the reign, and were three times more than the present average—even including those which are occasionally celebrated elsewhere than at the Parish Church.

It may also be interesting to notice, that in the year 1813 there were no funerals at Horsley after the middle of August to the end of the year, which fact would seem to indicate a very healthy time. The death rate for the following year, however, was unusually high.

The burial of the Rev. William Wilbraham is recorded in the year 1815.

In 1813, a new form for registering baptisms, marriages, and burials, came into operation in accordance with an Act of Parliament, passed in the preceding year, and this form—save in the case of marriages—is retained to the present day.

As now, the various entries were made after a printed form. There was no room for incidental notices of passing events, and from this time onward none occur.

GEORGE IV. REIGN—1820-1830.

A.D.	BAPTISMS.	WEDDINGS.	BURIALS.
1821.	73	26	32
1822.	76	38	37
1823.	64	36	49
1824.	76	39	34
1825.	80	44	40
1826.	77	38	48
1827.	59	32	37
1828.	68	24	40
1829.	65	16	42
1830.	49	30	37

WILLIAM IV. REIGN—1830.

1831.	59	28	37
1832.	69	26	55
1833.	68	27	39
1834.	68	25	42
1835.	72	22	30
1836.	81	18	47
1837.	164	19	71

QUEEN VICTORIA—1837.

1838.	42	10	77
1839.	46	11	31
1840.	53	15	44
1841.	51	18	41
1842.	36	12	36
1843.	39	21	31
1844.	53	11	44
1845.	30	12	37
1846.	36	12	49
1847.	32	10	36
1848.	17	11	43
1849.	54	9	35
1850.	72	17	36
1851.	57	11	37
1852.	48	10	44

A.D.	BAPTISMS.	WEDDINGS.	BURIALS.
1853.	97	13	40
1854.	49	13	42
1855.	70	15	45
1856.	68	10	42
1857.	54	16	34
1858.	50	18	35
1859.	65	11	33
1860.	57	14	38
1861.	59	7	46
1862.	49	13	20
1863.	46	8	27
1864.	40	4	36
1865.	39	11	24
1866.	32	12	29
1867.	28	11	25
1868.	62	8	29
1869.	43	15	22
1870.	52	11	34
1871.	85	11	32
1872.	91	14	41
1873.	53	9	37
1874.	51	12	35
1875.	43	13	31
1876.	49	3	30
1877.	37	4	42
1878.	25	9	24
1879.	34	6	27
1880.	35	10	26

In the years 1837 and '38 some very terrible epidemic must have prevailed in Horsley. The death-rate was exceedingly high for both those years, and a large number of children were amongst the dead. The effect of the calamity on the people generally is shown by the immense number of baptisms in the year 1837, and of adults as well as infants. In one week in the month of March, 1837, as many as 40 persons were baptised by the Rev. S. Lloyd, and during that year there was a total of 164 baptisms.

A note in the register records the fact that the foundation stone of the present Church was laid on March 29th, 1838, by the Vicar, the Rev. S. Lloyd; and the Church was consecrated on October 16th, 1839.

ST. MARTIN'S, HORSLEY.

The first baptism in the new Church was that of Emily Francis
Lloyd, on October 17th, the day after the consecration, who, in due
time, became the wife of a succeeding Vicar (the Rev. Vaughan S.
Fox), and is now living.

NOTES FOUND IN PARISH REGISTER, APPARENTLY IN THE
HAND-WRITING OF THE REV. DUDLEY FOSBROOK.

"1794. Oct. 19. The new Chapel of Nailsworth was opened by
the Rev. Anthony Keck, M.A., who thereupon resigned the
Curacy of this parish." Mr. Keck apparently was Curate again in
1811.

"Tradition says that the Rector of Avening was obliged originally
to find a Clergyman to do duty there once a day, and that there
were on this account frequent disputes between the inhabitants and
the Rectors. But there has been no duty done there in the memory
of the oldest person living—not even of Mrs. Elizabeth Castleman,
of Horsley, who died 1790, aged 99 years. The present Chapel is
supported by the profits of the pews. It is not consecrated."

"N.B. At a small distance, N.E. of the present Chapel, is the
shell of an ancient one, now used as a stable, in the occupation of
Mr. Blackwell, in which may still be seen the frame of the East
Window—a piscina—and entrance of rude workmanship in the
Gothic style. The arch of the windows is of the broader lancet
kind, 14th century."

To the above notes respecting Nailsworth Chapel, we may add
that Dudley Fosbrook says in his "History of Gloucestershire," "the
erection was principally owing to Jeremiah Day, Esq., the chief
inhabitant, who married the sister of John Remmington, Esq., of
Horsley." His additional statement, that "the Chapel is light and
elegant, and does credit to the architect, Mr. Dyer," is too great a
demand on our charity.

On another page of the same register is found the following
entry, "As there are the following blank leaves in this register,
which cannot be applied to the use for which it was designed, a
temptation is here thrown out to future Ministers, for the entertainment and perhaps service of posterity to record some memorandums
of the persons of respectability of whom this register contains any
account."

Then follow the entries as under:—

"The Rev. R. Davies, Vicar, who left his residence at this place
in consequence of being elected Vicar of Tetbury, by the Feoffees
thereof."

"Edward Wilbraham, Esq., second principal landed proprietor in the parish, whose estate and residence is in the tything of Nupend."

"Paul Castleman, Esq., Captain in the army. The house in which he resided at Barton End, was purchased after his decease by John Remmington, Esq., present inhabitant thereof."

"Rev. Robert Nicholl, Domestic Chaplain to the family at Chavenage House."

"Mrs. Elizabeth Castleman, widow, possessor of an estate at Nupend, which reverted after her death to Paul, son of above Paul Castleman, Esq., who settled it upon his wife, the present possessor (1797), though disputes still exist about it."

"The Hon. Margaret Castleman, sister of Lord Colville, wife of Captain Castleman. (She died October 25, 1794)."

"Mrs. Sarah Davis, of whose family see monuments in the Chancel and Burying Chapel; the farm belonging to her at Sugley where she removed, was purchased by a Mr. Townshend, of London."

"The estate of 300 acres of arable and pasture land, at and near Barton End, lately belonged to Thomas Pavey, of Woodchester, Esq., who died (1794 or 5), who left it on the decease of Mrs. Ann Pavey, and of his daughter, without issue, to his next heir, who is the George Pavey inserted in the baptisms of 1777. About 100 acres of these premises are tythe free, being demesne lands of the Abbey estate here."

"The great woods in this parish are the property of John Hugh Smith, Bart., of Long Ashton, in the county of Somerset."

"1799. Part of the property belonging to the Castleman family sold."

"1801. The estates of the Castleman family sold: the principal part of which was bought by the Rev. Mr. Keck." The Castlemans lived latterly at the old house called the Manor at Nup End. This house was pulled down by Mrs. McMullin and rebuilt some few years ago. The old oak staircase, said to be 300 years old, was preserved and placed in the new building.

SUNDRY NOTES FROM FOSBROOK'S HISTORY.

"Edward Wilbraham Esq., of Cirencester, and this place, a branch of the Cheshire Wilbrahams, who has been repeatedly nominated for High Sheriff of this county, Capt. Commandant of the Horsley Volunteers, B.A., University College, Oxford, has a pleasant summer mansion and a considerable estate here." The mansion was situated at the top of Nup End on the left hand. He

BARTON END HOUSE

had several children born and baptised at Horsley between the years 1784 and 1795.

"Edward Wood, Gentleman, Lieutenant of Marines, who married an Arundel of the Field, in Stroud, has an estate and good house at Horsley." It ought to be placed on record that the family has continued in possession until lately. The late Mrs. Wood, of Barton End, was one of the oldest inhabitants of Horsley. After a residence of 66 years she died in November, 1878.

"In the tithing of Barton End, a good estate is possessed by Mr. Henry Sheppard, a person of opulence, and an elegant mansion has been built by John Remmington, Esq., a Deputy-Lieutenant, descended from—Remmington, Lord Mayor of London, and great-grandson of George Smith, of the Nibley and Stonehouse family, High Sheriff for this county, 1710." This is the house now in the occupation of Major Williams, J.P. It was chiefly owing to the brother-in-law of this Mr. Remmington, Jeremiah Day, Esq., of Nailsworth, that the Nailsworth Church was built.

It is strange that Fosbrook makes no reference to the family of Castleman, members of which family left several benefactions for the poor of the parish. They seem to have preceded the Remmington family at Barton End. Bigland, in 1786 says, "At Barton End was the Barton for storing the corn rents belonging to the Abbey of Bruton. By the family of Webb it was bequeathed to Paul Castleman, Esq., and has since been purchased by John Remmington, gentleman. Certain manorial privileges are claimed by this tything." Bigland also says, "Very extensive beech woodlands, formerly called the Priors, are the property of Sir John Hugh Smith, Bart. This was the last property in the parish of Horsley which was sold by the family of Dennys."

HORSLEY CELEBRITIES.

Fosbrook says "The place has abounded with authors."

Samuel Hieron and Henry Stubbs and Fosbrook have been already noticed.

Another literary man of note was Mr. Jeremiah Jones, sometime Minister of Forest Green. He kept an Academy at Nailsworth, and was supposed to be the son of an opulent gentleman in the North of England. He received his education under his uncle, the Rev. Sam Jones — first of Gloucester, then of Tewkesbury — the tutor of Chandler, Butler, and Secker. He died in 1724.

Mr. Benjamin Francis, a Dissenting Minister at Shortwood, wrote some poems. He was the youngest son of Enoch Francis, a Baptist Minister in Wales; was educated at the Seminary in Bristol;

preached sometime at Sodbury, and removed to Horsley in 1757, where he died, December 14th, 1799.

Another was Miss Mary Deverell, unmarried daughter of a respectable clothier of this parish, who wrote some sermons.

Sydney Dobell is another of more recent date. He resided at Barton End House. He was the author of several poems. His "Life and Letters" have been published. He seems to have been delighted with his home at Barton End, which he called "a home to live and die in."

The following remarks, concerning his closing days at Barton End, are extracted from his "Life and Letters." To a friend he wrote: "We have here the rare privilege of being almost in mountain air, and with environments of such singular felicity as to defend us from the worst winds, and from that comparative sterility which usually makes residence at such a height too severe an optical asceticism. Barton End is an oasis of romantic beauty." In another letter he speaks of it as an earthly paradise, and says "the apple orchards are first now blossoming in the valley, and there's no cashmere of roses that can equal them." Through the first winter and early spring, spent at Barton End, some comparative health and vigour were gained, and he soon made himself felt as a beneficent influence in the new neighbourhood. The medical men ordered complete rest from mental exertion, but he could not and would not spare himself, and his overtaxed brain suffered severely. As his physical strength declined, through the spring and summer of 1873, his life was chiefly lived in his bedroom, and in a pretty little upstair sitting-room, the view from which towards the rookery delighted him.

On one of the early days in August he lay in his wife's invalid couch-carriage on the sunny gravel sweep in front of the house, taking his last fully conscious look at his beloved beech woods and the sloping terraced garden at the east end of the house of which he had always been especially fond.

In less than three weeks from that day, on the evening of August 22nd, 1874, as his favourite rooks making home were crossing the the sky in front of his windows, his last breath was quietly drawn. He was buried in the Cemetery at Painswick.

THE BAPTISTS AT SHORTWOOD.

A Baptist Meeting House was first opened at Shortwood in the year 1716.

The first Preacher of any note was Mr. Benjamin Francis, who came from Sodbury in 1757. In 1761 a house was built for him at

Tickmorend, at the junction of the two ways leading to the Fooks and Wallow Green. Here he resided until his death in 1799. He was succeeded by a Mr. Flint, who resigned his office of Preacher in 1803.

Next came the celebrated Mr. William Winterbotham. When formerly an assistant preacher at How's Lane Meeting, Plymouth, he preached two political sermons on Nov. 5th and 18th respectively, 1792, which brought him into great trouble. He was tried at Exeter, July 25, 1793, before Baron Perryn and a Special Jury, for exciting the King's subjects to sedition. The Jury returned a verdict of guilty, and in the following December "the very moderate and merciful sentence of Four years imprisonment and a Fine of Two Hundred Pounds" was passed upon him. He was imprisoned at Newgate.

It was in June, 1802, Mr. Winterbotham first preached at Shortwood, and in April, 1804, he became the appointed Minister. It is no wonder that a man with such a history became a source of great attraction. He continued Minister at Shortwood until 1829, when he died. He was succeeded from 1832 to 1865 by Mr. Newman.

The Chapel was rebuilt in 1838, and was pulled down again in 1882 and removed to Nailsworth.

The following passages taken from "A Brief Narrative of the Life and Death of Mr. Benjamin Francis" give an idea of the of the appearance of the Shortwood Valley in the middle of the last Century.—"The Meeting house was built between two hills surrounded with woods and a few scattered houses ; for at that time the neighbourhood was far from being populous, though the great increase in the Cloathing business has made an alteration since."

"Any friend of evangelical religion must have enjoyed the sight of the several companies descending the surrounding hills on the Lord's Day to assemble at Shortwood; where, on the rising ground above the Meeting House, one group after another would appear emerging from the woods ; some of them coming from ten miles distance and upwards."

ALL SAINTS' CHURCH, SHORTWOOD.

This building was erected during the time in which the Rev. Vaughan S. Fox was Vicar of Horsley, and was consecrated by the Bishop of Gloucester and Bristol on May 26th, 1866. It stands on the site of the old dilapidated poorhouse, in which a weekly evening service had been held for many years, and which it had become necessary to sell. The money required was raised by private sub-

scriptions, assisted by grants from the Warneford Trustees and the
Diocesan Society,—a friend having generously provided the means
for the purchase of the site. Mr. Clissold, of Stroud, was the
architect, and Mr. E. Clayfield, of Horsley, the builder. The
Church accommodates 200 persons, and the seats were all free and
unappropriated. On the occasion of the consecration of the
Church by Bishop Ellicott (who preached from St. John v. 6), the
building was beautifully decorated with leaves, flowers, and illumin-
ated texts, and after the service a luncheon was given in a tent on
the Vicarage lawn to the Bishop and many of the clergy and gentry
of the neighbourhood, 70 in all, when some interesting speeches
were made by the Bishop and others. The choir had a luncheon
provided for them at the Vicarage Farm. After the death of the
Rev. Vaughan S. Fox a number of his clerical brethren expressed
their wish to erect some remembrance of him, the form of the
memorial being left to his widow, who chose a tablet to be placed
in All Saints' Church, the building of which was the fulfilment
of his earnest desires and long-cherished plans for the good of
that portion of Horsley Parish in which it is situated.

STRAY NOTES.

Tradition says that in the coaching days there stood an Inn at
Barton End, known as "The Bell," which was situated a little
above Barton End House, on the right hand side. Some of the
coaches changed horses at "Tipput's Inn," and some at "The
Bell." The horse-trough, belonging to the latter, is said to be
still in its place, but is partially covered over.

The Itinerary says (see page 4) "In Horsley, Nailsworth, Inchborough, and Rodborough the clothing manufacture is carried on to a
great extent. They are only villages, but they are in population equal
to considerable towns. Near Inchborough is Spring Park, a seat
of Lord Ducie; near Rodborough is Hill House, a seat of Sir
George Onesiphorous Paul."

It then goes on to say that "Gloucestershire was divided into 30
hundreds, about the year 890, by King Alfred. In these hundreds
are found one city, Gloucester, two borough towns which send
members to Parliament, viz., Cirencester and Tewkesbury, and 26
other towns where weekly markets are held," and Horsley is mentioned as one.

The Horsley Market appears to have been held at the bottom of
Horsley Street, and probably opposite the present Boot Inn.
The old Market Cross, or rather what remains of it, is built into

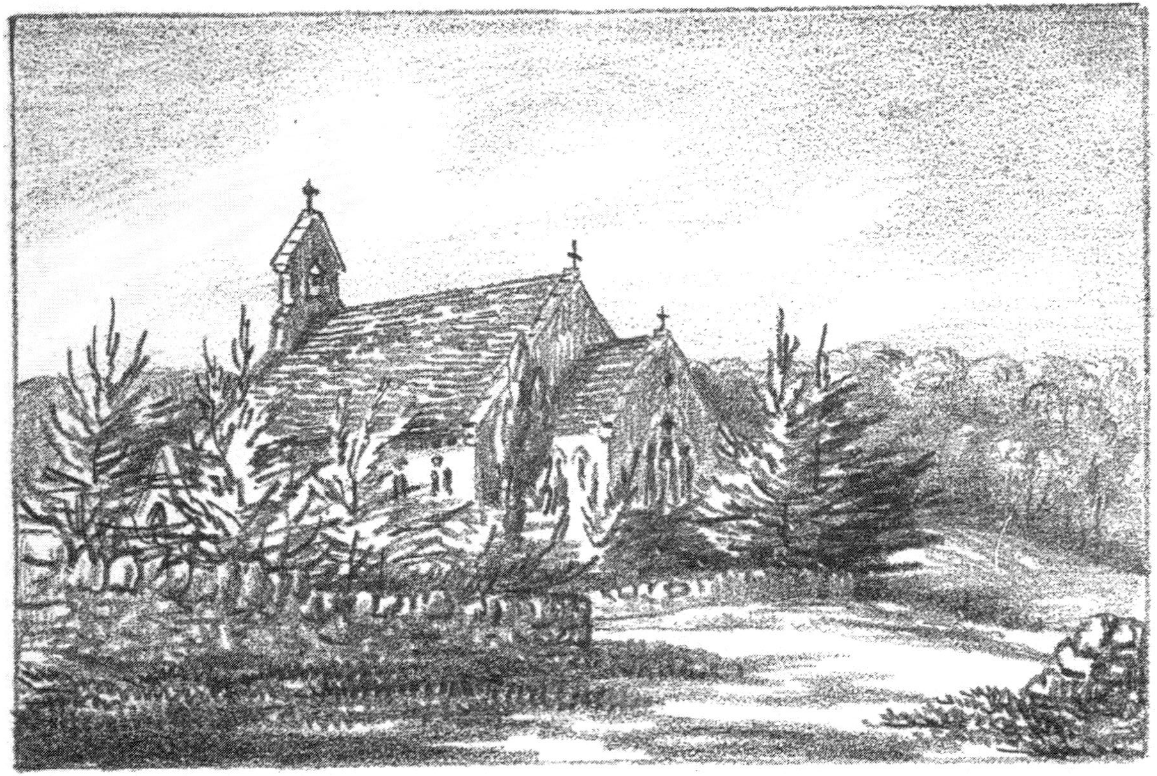

ALL SAINTS', SHORTWOOD.

the steps of the hay-loft, or granary, between the Bell Inn and the Churchyard. It stood, originally, somewhere by the corner opposite the Boot Inn. "Standing on the cross" is a phrase still used by some and applies to the corner before named.

The population of various places in the neighbourhood is also given, as Minchinhampton, which contained, in 1801, 3,419 persons, Tetbury, 2,500; Cirencester, 4,130; Dursley, 2,379; Stroud, 5422; Painswick, 3,150; Gloucester, 7579.

The population of Horsley, 40 years ago, was estimated to be about 4,000, for this is the number given by the Rev. S. Lloyd, in a circular issued by him when soliciting aid for the rebuilding of the Church. The same circular shows that the post-town was Chalford.

The Itinerary states, "During the season a coach runs from Cheltenham to Bath every Tuesday and Friday; and from Bath to Cheltenham every Wednesday and Saturday." The London coaches ran at the rate of "5½ miles an hour," those on "the cross roads at the rate of 5 miles, including stops."

There is also an incidental mention that "rugs and blankets were made at Nailsworth, Dursley, and other clothing towns."

At the breaking out of the French War at the close of the last century, a corps of Volunteers was raised in Horsley. Mr. Wilbraham was the "Commandant" for a period of ten years. Mr. Daniel Smith, gentleman, was appointed to the Lieutenancy in 1803, and to the Captaincy in 1807.

The parchments conferring these latter appointments were exhibited at the late Horsley Exhibition, and are in the possession of Mr. Alfred Smith, Solicitor, of Nailsworth.

THE CENSUS OF THE PARISH OF HORSLEY, 1881.

Enumeration District.	Inhabited Houses.	No. of Separate Families.
1.—Part of the parish of Horsley, lying South South-East, comprising Chavenage, Ledgemore, Cranmore, Sandgrove, Tiltup's End, including Turnpike Gate and cottage the Nailsworth side of it, and Hay Lane to the Brook at Hartley Bridge	35	35
2.—Part of the parish of Horsley, lying South-West, comprising Sugley, Hollingham, part of Tickmorend, Parsonage House, Wallow Green, Lophorn, Lower and Upper Luther-		

Enumeration District.	Inhabited Houses.	No. of Separate Families.
idge, Twatley, Lutsome, Ragged, Dolly, Nelmes, Boscombe, and Nup End, including the Manor House	50	50
3.—Part of the parish of Horsley, lying South, comprising Upper and Lower Barton End, Davis' Mill, Washpond to the Stream, Windmill Cottage, Windsor Ash, including Barcelona and Harley Wood.	68	68
4.—Part of the Parish of Horsley, lying North, comprising Newmarket, Tinkley Gate Cottage, Kingley Bottom Cottages, under the High Wood, Bittom Wood, Whorley, The Lot, including Mr. Rotton's house	63	63
5.—Part of the Parish of Horsley, lying South, comprising Horsley, Hartley Bridge to the Stream, Coldwell, Wormwood Hill, and all the Cottages the Horsley side of the Stream at Down End	72	72
6.—Part of the parish of Horsley, lying South, comprising Down End, Upper and Lower Drawley Hill, including Cottages occupied by Messrs. Park, Webb, Worthy Drew, R. Holmes, The Vicarage, and Fooks	78	69
7.—Part of the parish of Horsley, lying South-East, comprising Shortwood Green, Wag Hill, Botley's Court, Node's Cottages, to the Brook, Walkley Wood, including P. Dyer and Jack of the Nick	74	68
8.—Part of the parish of Horsley, lying South-East, comprising Nailsworth, including Clutterbuck's Mill, Barn Close, Chestnut Hill, and Ringfield House	107	105
9.—Part of the parish of Horsley, lying East, comprising Rockness Hill, Mount Hor, Tucking Cross, Steps, Millbottom Mills and Walkley's Cottages in Bath Road, including Playne's Mill and William Barnfield	66	66

Districts.	Separate Families.	Houses Inhabited.	Houses Unin- habited.	Building.	Persons Males.	Females.	Totals.
1	35	33	2	—	85	86	171
2	58	50	8	—	95	106	201
3	68	68	7	—	119	150	269
4	63	62	5	—	116	161	277
5	72	72	8	—	132	147	279
6	78	69	9	—	161	154	315
7	74	68	3	—	141	143	284
8	107	105	8	—	202	276	478
9	66	66	3	—	126	137	263
Totals....	621	593	53	None	1177	1360	2537

THE CONTENTS OF THE PARISH CHEST.

The old Parish Chest, which for many years stood under the stairs in the Tower, contains chiefly a series of old Parish Account Books, beginning with Oct. 14th, 1765, and ending May, 1836.

As a rule, the entries are of no interest, but occasionally there occurs an entry which may be worth recording for the entertainment of old parishioners.

"At a Vestry Meeting held this 18th day of December, 1766, by the Churchwardens and Overseers of the Poor, and others, the inhabitants of the Parish of Horsley, in the County of Gloucester, after notice given in the Church for that purpose on Sunday last, it is unanimously agreed by us whose names are under written, that the cottages, the property of the parish be disposed of by public auction, on Thursday, the 15th day of January next, between the hours of twelve and four, at the dwelling-house of Robert Wilkins, known by the sign of the Star, in the said parish, and that the money arising by such sale to be disposed of towards making the present Workhouse tenantable for the aged poor.

W. G. CHAMBERS, } Churchwardens.

STEPHEN TEAKLE, } Overseers.
WM. KEMP,

"Also at a Vestry Meeting held 5th October, 1776.............. it was unanimously agreed...that three waggon loads of wheat be bought by the officers of the parish for the use of the poor. That the same is to be made into bread at ten pounds for one shilling, and sold to the poor at that price. And farther, it is agreed that the officers are to be indemnified by the poor rate for every

F

extraordinary expense that may attend the buying, bringing home, and baking the same.''

"At a Vestry meeting held this 8th day of July, 1765, we, whose names are here under-written, do unanimously agree to subscribe two guineas annually towards the support of the Bath Hospital.''

THOS. BLACKWELL, } Churchwardens.

WM. COX GRIFFITHS, } Overseers.

"At a Vestry meeting held this 27th day of July, 1766, it is agreed by Mr. Thos. Clarke and Jno. Kemmish, they being the only persons who attended the Vestry except the officers, that Mr. Gardener be employed by the parish in the prosecution of Jno. Harvey for the murder of his wife, and in case Mr. Gardener finds it necessary, to fee a counsel against him at Gloucester.''

Perhaps he saved them the trouble by committing suicide, for there is a spot known on the Bath Road as Harvey's grave.

Again. "At a Vestry meeting this 31st day of March, 1766, we, whose names are here-under written, do unanimously agree to pay the sum of three pounds, ten shillings, and sixpence, for the expense of repairing the late Shipton's seat, and giving the same seat to Mr. John Harvey in full recompense for his right to his former seat now inclosed in the Minister's Desk.''

JOSEPH BROWNING, } Churchwardens.
THOS. BLACKWELL, }

THOS. WILKINS,
WM. COX GRIFFITHS, } Overseers.
ETC , ETC. }

"April 4th, 1768. Whereas we whose names are here unto sub-scribed being met pursuant to the notice given for that purpose and having duly weighed and considered the great utility that is likely to attend the building of a new Workhouse in this parish, do agree that Mr. John Gillman, Mr. Thos. Pavey, and Mr. Stephen Wilkins, shall make a survey of a proper place for erecting the same, and make a report thereof to the next Vestry, with a plan for building the same, and if approved of, the officers to begin building the same as soon as convenient.''

GEORGE GWINNETT,   R. STEPHENS,
JNO. WALLIS,   ROBT. STEPHENS,
JNO. HARVEY,   EDW. SMYTH,
ETC.,   ETC.

Very expedite were these gentlemen in making their survey and report, as the next entry shows.

"April 14th, 1768. This day at a Vestry held for that purpose, Mr. Stephen Wilkins, Mr. Thos. Pavey, and Mr. Jno. Gillman, have, agreeable to an order of a Vestry made the 4th inst., made a survey of a proper place for erecting a Workhouse on Shortwood Green: a plan whereof was this day delivered by them and approved of by the Vestry, and it is unanimously agreed that the said Workhouse shall be built according to the said plan and at the expense of the parish, and to be carried on with all speed, and do nominate Mr. Thos. Pavey, Mr. John Gillman, and John Harvey, agents for erecting the same, and do allow the above agents to borrow on interest two hundred pounds for the above present use."

ROBT. STEPHENS	JOSEPH BROWNING,
GEO. GWINNETT,	W. CHAMBERS,

ETC.

The original Workhouse appears to have been situated somewhere near "Horsley Cross."

Some further notices occur respecting the building of the Workhouse at Shortwood, but are of no particular interest.

Then to the same year belongs the following:—"Agreed at a Vestry held the 8 day of October, 1768, by us, that the Constables of this parish shall be paid their reasonable expenses in taking Distressis (sic) on the Ale-house Keepers as convicted for selling ale without a license, and we, whose names are under written, are determined they shall be prosecuted at the expense of this parish with all speed."

ROBT. STEPHENS,	THOS. PAVEY,
JOSEPH BUTTER,	JNO. GILLMAN,
GEO. GWINNETT,	DAN. WALKLEY,
ETC.,	ETC.

"1770.—At a Vestry held this 17th day of May, agreeable to notice given, it is agreed that two substantial persons, having no connection with this parish, shall be nominated and appointed to take a general survey of the parish by a future Vestry to be held some reasonable time before Easter next, and at the said Vestry two persons of this parish shall be nominated to assist the Surveyors and all at the expense of this parish. R. Stephens, &c., &c."

"1771.—At a Vestry held this 21st of March, agreeable to notice given in Church, it is agreed–That Joseph Pavey, Samuel Remington, Thomas Clutterbuck, and Joshua Thomas, be chosen to take a

F 2

general survey of this parish, and that the present Overseers doo
apply to the above gentlemen, and that two of them doo survey the
whole parish as soon as possible, and its further agreed that Jno.
Harvey and Thomas Clark doo show to the above chosen all lands,
and give them all proper information thereon, and all the expenses
attending to be paid by the parish.

Wm. Wallis, ⎫ Churchwardens.   Step. Wilkins, ⎫ Overseers.
Wm. Frost, ⎭   William Skammell, ⎭

ETC.

Sometimes the Vestry acted the part of a Charity Organisation
Society, as the following indicates:—

"Lent, Oct. 22, 1770.   John Smith, a Loome for the support of
himselfe and famlyee, which belongs to the parish, by Mr. William
Deverell, Overseer."

"At a Vestry meeting held this 10th day of May, 1771, it is
agreed for the Workhouse to be farmed, and an advertisement to be
inserted in the next *Gloucester Journal.*

Robert Stephens,
Thomas Wight."

"Lett a house to Saml. Teakle, of Shortwood, at £1 16s. per
annum, the rent to commence from Dec. 25, 1770.   This house was
Edward Box's, and delivered up to keep his son Joshua in the
Workhouse, May 7th, 1771.

"At a Vestry held this 14th day of August, 1772, it is ordered
and agreed by us, whose names are underwritten, being the Churchwardens and Overseers of the Poor of the parish of Horsley, and
others of the most substantial inhabitants, that those people who
receive constant monthly pay from this parish, shall immediately
after next pay day be all sent to the Workhouse, or receive no more
relief."

"A memorandum made this 12th day of April, 1773, between
Mr. Jno. Gillman, of Horsley, and the inhabitants of the same
parish, viz.:—the said Jno. Gillman do agree with us, whose names
are underwritten, and all other payers to the poor rates of the said
parish, to take and farm all the poor of the said parish for one year
at the sum of eight hundred and fifty pounds, which sum is to be
raised on the estates in the said parish, according to articles to be
made for the above purpose between Mr. Jno. Gillman and the
inhabitants on the 22nd inst.   Further the said Jno. Gillman is

from this day to take the poor on the account of the sum of eight hundred and fifty pounds."

GEORGE GWINNETT,	JNO. GILLMAN,
JOHN LEVERSAGE,	ROBT. STEPHENS,
WM. WALLIS,	THOM. WRIGHT,
ETC.	ETC.

THE SCHOOLS.

Copied from a tablet which was formerly placed in Horsley School.

"In the year 1744, Edward Webb, by his will, gave £200 to four trustees, viz.:—Paul Castleman, the Rev. Richard Wallington, John Wood, and Thomas Butler, to be applied for the Benefit of the parish of Horsley."

"In 1752, Mrs. Castleman, sister of the above named Edward Webb, gave £200 to four trustees, viz.:—Paul Castleman her husband, Thos. Butler, Rev. Richard Wallington, and Richard Stephens, to be invested in the purchase of freehold land and tenements for the endowment of a Free School, in which poor children of the parish of Horsley were to be taught to read, write, and cast accounts, and also to learn the Church Catechism. A person of the Established Church of England was to be appointed master, and to be removed, and another elected at the discretion of the trustees. The master to be paid the money arising from the lands after deducting taxes, payments, and repairs. In 1775, Mr. Castleman gave £50."

"In 1788, Mrs. Anne Wight, of Tetbury, by her will, gave to her nephew, Edward Wilbraham, and to the trustees of the Horsley Free School, £100 for the benefit of the said School. Mr. Henry Stephens gave £50, and Mrs. Sarah Wilbraham £30 for the same purpose; all which monies have been invested in land as they thought proper."

"In 1817, Mr. Henry Shepherd, of Barton End, granted and endowed for the benefit of the Free School a close of pasture land in the Tything of Tickmorend, containing 1 acre 17 perches, with the Tithe, &c., and Miss Mary Frost, sister-in-law of the said Henry Shepherd, gave £100 for the same charitable purpose. In 1823, Thos. Wilkins the late master died, and it was thought expedient to   the School upon the National System, and to erect a new School-room, the old School building being ruinous, and totally inadequate for the purpose. The National Society granted £80, and the Diocesan Society £20 towards the building, &c.,

and the remainder of the expense £130 was raised by subscriptions, of which E. Wilbraham, Esq., gave £50. The first stone was laid July 30th, 1823, and the School was opened March 30th, 1824. The present trustees are E. Wilbraham. senr., W. B. Smith, James Young, and E. Wilbraham, junr. This table was erected in the year 1827."

The following notices are gathered chiefly from the minute book :

In the year 1863 the interest of £300 was left by the late Edward Wilbraham, Esq., Q.C., for the benefit of the Horsley Church School.

In 1864, the old School House, which was situated at Tickmor-End on the School Ground, just opposite the turning which leads to Wallow Green, was pulled down, and the shed which now occupies the site was erected apparently out of the materials.

In 1866, a further endowment was given as the following interest-ing entry shows—"At a Meeting held at Horsley Vicarage, on Tuesday, November 20th, the School trustees having been informed of the intention of the Rev. W. H. Bathurst to devote a sum of money towards the endowment of the parish Schools, resolved, that their best thanks be offered to Mr. Bathurst for his liberality, and that Mr. Bathurst be informed of their willingness to administer the funds in such manner as he may direct." This indeed was a handsome gift, for the interest yields the yearly sum of £46 1s. 8d. And the above is not all that was done by this liberal-hearted Clergyman for the benefit of the Horsley School.

In 1868, another entry occurs which tells of a further sum of £100 set aside by Mr. Bathurst, for the purchase of a suitable house for the master ; of a piece of land for the boy's playground, if a favourable opportunity of buying such property presented itself; meanwhile, the interest to go into the School Fund.

In 1869, the purchase of a house for the schoolmaster's residence, and of a piece of land for a boy's playground, was completed by the Rev. N. Cornford acting as representative of the trustees of the School, by their consent. The vendor was Thomas Henry Bird. The expense, £117 10s. 0d., was defrayed by the £100 of Mr. Bathurst, with interest, £4 1s. 3d., and other voluntary contributions.

The annual income from endowment is as follows :

	£	s.	d.
The Bathurst charity	46	1	8*
Charity commissioners	18	2	2
Rent of land, consisting of a field at Lutsom, one at Twotley, two fields at Tickmorend, and one above the Vicarage, known as the Ridings	49	10	0
TOTAL....	£113	13	10

The trustees of the School are:—Henry Pavey, Esq., Charles Playne, Esq., Major Williams, J.P., Rev. M. Rudkin, General Horsley, and Mr. G. Blackwell.

OTHER BENEFACTIONS.

The following are taken from Rudder and Bigland's Histories.

"The. Rev. Henry Stubbs (time unknown), gave £20, vested in Mrs. Castleman, the interest to be laid out in purchasing testaments for the poor."

"In 1714, Walter Chambers gave £10, vested as above, the interest to be laid out in bread for the poor."

"In 1770, Joseph Browning gave by will moneys vested in William Smith, the interest of which is to buy testaments for the poor."

Some of the testament money has been lost, but in what way no one can now tell. The testament money, arising from the field called the Testament Ground, has for many years amounted to only £1. The following are the particulars of the sale of this field, in 1850, which was the property of Admiral Young:

"A close of freehold pasture land, called the Testament Ground, containing 5A. 0R. 9P. This close was previously to Admiral Young's purchase, subject, along with other property, to a rent of £3 payable to the Churchwardens and Overseers of the Poor of the parish of Horsley, and of which sum, 20s. has been, since the Admiral's purchase, paid by him in respect of this Lot. The purchaser is therefore to take this Lot subject to the last mentioned annual payment, and is not to require any proof of exemption from or indemnity against the payment of the residue of the £3."

As regards the Walter Chamber's bread charity, no one now seems to know anything about it. But as late as 1861 there is an entry in a parish book—"Rent of land, given in bread by A. Fewster, 10/-"

---

* By subsequent permission this money may be applied for the use and benefit of the Schools—not exclusively for the Infant School. NOTE IN PARISH BOOK.

At a later date, 1868, occurs a similar entry:
"10/- Bread. Lower Mead Splash Meadow, near Hope Cottage, above Walkley Wood—? Dec^r., Mrs. A. Fewster, Nailsworth."

The following Charity Moneys are paid yearly by the Charity Commissioners.

	£	s.	d.	
Col. Ollney's Charity	9	12	2	Administered by Churchwardens
Sheppard's Charity (including Frost's).	17	9	10	and Overseers.

The above Charities are expended in providing coats for 11 poor men, and cloaks for 8 poor women who (in both cases) are not in receipt of parish relief. The remainder of the money is expended in blankets.

Wilbraham's Charity for blankets for the poor—£9, administered by Trustees of School.

Wight's Bread Charity—£1 7s. 8d., administered by Overseers.

Total of above Charities—£37 9s. 8d.

THE MILLS.

There was a watermill in Horsley in the days of Edward the Confessor. It was worth at that time £12. And when Domesday was compiled, 1084, it was valued at £14. One would like to know where that old mill stood, for it was evidently the first of the many mills which to-day cover our streams.

It would also be interesting to know when the weaving was first introduced into the parish. Some of the local names, said to be of Flemish origin, indicate an early date. Farmilo, a name which is common, it is said, used to be spelt Flanderho, and was given in contempt of the foreigners, to whom it afterwards became affixed. I feel bound to say, however, that our parish registers afford no proof of this. And Farmilo does not appear to have been a very early name in the parish.

Rudder says, 1779. "The clothing business hath encouraged great numbers of families to settle here, but manufacture declining of late, the poor are very burthensome for way of employment; but much of their wretched condition is owing to idleness and bad habits." Then shortly after trade revived. An entry in the register by Dudley Fosbrook says, "1796, The new mills near the Washpond, made upon the estate lately belonging to Miss Deveralls, of Nailsworth, but purchased by John Remmington, gentleman."

Then another entry reads, "1800. The new Turnpike Road and Mr. Smith's Mill begun."

So it seems from these notices that in the old times there were fluctuations in the clothing business, and at the close of another century, one has to speak of the clothing manufacture as having declined of late. But as at the close of the last century there was a great revival as to necessitate the building of more mills, so let us hope that now in the immediate future, there may be an increase of trade and prosperity to the parish such as it has never experienced before.

We are sorry to have to record that in consequence of the want of employment many of the inhabitants have had to leave the parish during the last three years, and many have emigrated. These emigrants have gone to many parts of the world, but chiefly to the United States, Canada, The Cape, New Zealand, and Australia. A large number went, in 1883, to Brisbane. On their departure the Vicar sent a letter of commendation to the Bishop of Brisbane and received the following interesting reply:

"Bishopsbourne,

Brisbane,

Sept. 25, 1883.

My Dear Sir,

It is pleasant to me to receive a letter from my old neighbourhood; although, your letter is one of the many reminders which I receive from time to time, that I have nearly outlived my generation. That an Incumbent of Horsley should have risen up who knows nothing about me, but what he gathers from the Clergy List, is a significant fact. Nearly 44 years ago, *i.e.*, towards the end of 1839, I was the preacher in your Church upon some great occasion, when the Bishop (Monk) and a number of Clergy were present.

I think it must have been the re-opening of the Church after repairs, or something of that sort. I do not remember what the occasion was.[1] I was just at that time entering upon the Incumbency of Stroud, and I held that Incumbency until the latter end of 1845.

. . . .

I have handed your letter about your emigrants to the Clergyman, who usually looks after new comers. 'The Duke of Westminster'

---

1 The occasion was the opening of the Church after re-erection.

arrived 2 or 3 weeks ago; but the immigrants have been in quarantine; and they are landing only to-day. . . . . . .

Matthew B. Hale,
Bishop."

Thus Horsley is gradually being denuded of its inhabitants. Probably quite 300 souls have left the parish since the census of 1881. The parish has had a long and to some of us an interesting history—though it has been always a poor place. We wish for it a prosperous and happy future. Nothing could be better either for the parish itself or its neighbourhood than a revival of its ancient cloth manufactures. We should like to see its healthy and picturesque valleys well filled with a prosperous and contented people. But if its manufactures should not return, then perhaps it may become a place of resort, a favourite residence for those who have done their work elsewhere and wish for rest amidst exceedingly salubrious and picturesque surroundings.

FINIS.

WHITMORE AND SON, LETTERPRESS AND LITHOGRAPHIC PRINTERS, DURSLEY.

Lightning Source UK Ltd.
Milton Keynes UK
UKHW020702090223
416722UK00005B/486

9 781354 513996